# AMERICAN ORIGINS
## *of Churches of Christ*

THREE ESSAYS
ON RESTORATION HISTORY

I0798772

RICHARD HUGHES
NATHAN O. HATCH
DAVID EDWIN HARRELL, JR.

*with introduction and analysis by*
DOUGLAS A. FOSTER

American Origins of Churches of Christ: Three Essays on Restoration History

ACU
PRESS

ACU Station, Box 29138
Abilene, TX 79699

Cover design and typesetting by Tigris Creative Studios, LLC, Fort Worth, Texas.
www.tigrisstudios.com

*Permissions*

Nathan O. Hatch. "The Christian Movement and the Demand for a Theology of the People," © 1987, by the *Journal of American History*. Reprinted by permission of the Organization of American Historians.

David Edwin Harrell, Jr. "The Sectional Origins of Churches of Christ," © 1964, by the Southern Historical Association. Reprinted from the *Journal of Southern History* by permission of the Managing Editor.

Richard T. Hughes. "The Apocalyptic Origins of Churches of Christ and the Triumph of Modernism," © 1992, by the Center for the Study of Religion and American Culture. Reprinted from *Religion and American Culture*, by permission.



Printed in the United States of America

ISBN 0-89112-0092

Library of Congress Card Number **99-66740**

**3,4,5**

# Table of Contents

# ACKNOWLEDGEMENTS

**Richard T. Hughes**

The core of this small book is a collection of three essays, each exploring the origins of the Churches of Christ in the United States from a different angle. In 1964, David Edwin Harrell Jr. published the first of these essays in the *Journal of Southern History* under the title, "The Sectional Origins of the Churches of Christ." In this groundbreaking essay, Harrell argued that one cannot understand the emergence of Churches of Christ in the early nineteenth century apart from southern sectionalism, rural isolation, and poverty. Then, in 1980, *The Journal of American History* published another pioneering essay, this one by Nathan O. Hatch entitled, "The Christian Movement and the Demand for a Theology of the People." For Hatch, the origins of Churches of Christ are rooted in the democratization of American culture and religion in the early nineteenth century. Finally, in 1992 Richard Hughes published in *Religion and American Culture* an essay entitled "The Apocalyptic Origins of Churches of Christ and the Triumph of Modernism." Hughes located the origins of Churches of Christ in the apocalyptic orientation best represented in the nineteenth century by Barton W. Stone and David Lipscomb.

Each of these essays was an attempt to explore in succinct form what the authors sought to develop in greater detail in subsequent books. Harrell developed his "sectional origins" thesis in *Quest for a Christian America: The Disciples of Christ and American Society to 1866* (Disciples of Christ Historical Society, 1966). Hatch developed his "democratization" thesis in *The Democratization of American Christianity* (Yale, 1989). Hughes developed his "apocalyptic" thesis in *Reviving the Ancient Faith: The Story of Churches of Christ in America* (Eerdmans, 1996).

The authors gratefully acknowledge *The Journal of*

*Southern History, The Journal of American History,* and *Religion and American Culture,* in which the essays were originally published, for their permission to republish them in this form. Thanks also to ACU Press for bringing together in one volume these three essays.

I am grateful to John Richter and especially to Krystin Higgins, both graduate students in religion at Pepperdine University, for help in preparing this material for the publisher.

# INTRODUCTION

Douglas A. Foster

Without question the essays in this volume are landmarks in the historiography and self-understanding of the Stone-Campbell Movement, especially Churches of Christ. Written by two insiders and one outsider, each reflects significant developments in Stone-Campbell studies in the last forty years. All three pieces were written originally for consumption by professional historians and together form a solid collection for use in university and seminary courses in Stone-Campbell and American religious history. Yet the authors are all wonderful storytellers who articulate their material clearly and engagingly, making the material suitable for audiences in many settings, including church classes and small group discussions.

Nathan Hatch's work is one of the most important pieces of intellectual history ever written on the movement. Though not the only "outsider" to take note of this religious reform effort[1], the fact that such a careful and discerning historian of American religion portrayed it as representative of major trends in American religion provided impetus for other studies concerning the movement's relationship to the larger American culture.[2] Hatch shows the Stone and Campbell movements to be prime examples of what in his 1989 book he would label the "democratization" of American Christianity.[3] This populist emphasis on the absolute freedom (and ability) of individuals to understand the Bible for themselves without

---

[1]See Richard Tristano, *The Origins of the Restoration Movement: An Intellectual History* (Atlanta, Georgia: Glenmary Research Center, 1988).

[2]Richard T. Hughes and C. Leonard Allen, *Illusions of Innocence: Protestant Primitivism in America, 1630-1875* (Chicago: University of Chicago Press, 1988).

[3]*The Democratization of American Christianity* (New Haven: Yale University Press, 1989). See also "Millennialism and Popular Religion in the Early Republic," in *The Evangelical Tradition in America*, 113-130 (Macon: Mercer University Press, 1984).

benefit of clergy was certainly not a new idea.[4] Hatch tied these sentiments of the movement to the larger cultural upheavals in American society in the late eighteenth and early nineteenth centuries, showing the movement's major role in the development of popular religion in the United States.

David Edwin Harrell Jr., a life-long member of Churches of Christ, provided in his 1964 essay the first scholarly explanation of the largely southern origins and character of Churches of Christ. This essay along with Harrell's other early work on the movement[5] sparked the imagination of a generation of scholars in Churches of Christ at a time of great upheaval in that body's perceptions of itself. Though remaining a theological conservative and loyal member of that religious heritage, Harrell carefully demonstrated that "we" had developed out of specific historic circumstances. His work challenged a long-held taboo in Churches of Christ—admitting that our beliefs and practices had indeed been shaped in many ways by the social, cultural, and economic circumstances of our American context. Its publication in the respected *Journal of Southern History* served to enhance its credibility and impact.

An interesting secondary indication of the development of Stone-Campbell studies in the late twentieth century is evident in Harrell's consistent use of "Disciples" as the name of the movement. In the nineteenth century that was one of the most commonly used designations for the entire movement. During the first part of the twentieth century most histories of the movement were written by scholars from the segment known most often as Disciples, in distinction from Churches of Christ. The label was used almost exclusively in scholarly writing, though "Restoration Movement" was still more common in the popular press. Since the publication of

---

[4]See Ronald E. Osborn, *Experiment in Liberty: The Ideal of Freedom in the Experience of the Disciples of Christ*, The Forrest F. Reed Lectures for 1976 (St. Louis: The Bethany Press, 1978).

[5]David Edwin Harrell, Jr., "Disciples of Christ Pacifism in Nineteenth Century Tennessee," *Tennessee Historical Quarterly* 21 (September 1962) 263-274; "The Agrarian Myth and the Disciples of Christ in the Nineteenth Century," *Agricultural History* 41 (April 1967) 181-192; "Peculiar People: A Rationale for Modern Conservative Disciples," in *Disciples and the Church Universal*, The Reed lectures for 1966 (Nashville: Disciples of Christ Historical Society, 1967) 34-44.

the first edition of Leroy Garrett's history *The Stone-Campbell Movement* in 1981, the label "Disciples" as well as "Restoration Movement" are gradually being replaced by the term "Stone-Campbell Movement" in scholarly publications.[6]

Richard Hughes, like Harrell, a lifetime member of Churches of Christ, has provided in his essay the seeds for what some would label the first truly critical history of Churches of Christ.[7] In this article Hughes tests the thesis he would develop more completely in the book: first, that Churches of Christ were the legitimate heirs of what he designates "Stoneite apocalypticism." This was characterized by a strong sense of the sovereignty of God and the tenuous and temporary nature of earthly existence. Second, however, Hughes posits that the group lost this worldview in stages during the twentieth century, accommodating itself to "modernistic" views focusing on human reason and ability.

Hughes has been a major interpreter of Stone-Campbell history for both internal and external audiences for over two decades. Much of his work has focused on the movement's primitivism, often comparing it to other manifestations of religious primitivism and restorationism.[8] In this essay he continues that trajectory but in a much more detailed and nuanced manner. Here he delineates two kinds of primitivism that he labels rationalistic postmillennial

---

[6]Leroy Garrett, *The Stone-Campbell Movement: An Anecdotal History of Three Churches* (Joplin, Missouri: College Press Pub. Co., 1981); *The Stone-Campbell Movement: The Story of the American Restoration Movement* (Joplin, Missouri: College Press Pub. Co., 1994). The forthcoming *Encyclopedia of the Stone-Campbell Movement* is another indication of the standardization of the term.

[7]*Reviving the Ancient Faith: The Story of Churches of Christ in America* (Grand Rapids: Wm. B. Eerdmans Publishing Company, 1996).

[8]See for example "A Comparison of the Restitution Motifs of the Campbells (1809-1830) and the Anabaptists (1524-1560)," *Mennonite Quarterly Review* 45 (October 1971):312-30; "From Primitive Church to Civil Religion: The Millennial Odyssey of Alexander Campbell," *Journal of the American Academy of Religion* 44 (March 1976):87-103; "The Role of Theology in the Nineteenth Century Division of Disciples of Christ," in *American Religion: 1974 Proceedings*, 56-78, ed. Edwin S. Gaustad (Tallahassee, Florida: American Academy of Religion, 1974); and C. Leonard Allen, *Discovering Our Roots: The Ancestry of Churches of Christ* (Abilene: ACU Press, 1988); editor, *The American Quest for the Primitive Church* (Urbana: University of Illinois Press, 1988); "Reclaiming a Heritage," *Restoration Quarterly* 37 (Third Quarter, 1995):129-138; editor, *The Primitive Church in the Modern World* (Urbana: University of Illinois Press, 1995.

primitivism and apocalyptic premillennial primitivism, epitomized respectively by Alexander Campbell and Barton W. Stone. Hughes explains that although some readers have confused the stances of the two leaders (whose views sometimes overlap in specifics), the two ideas came apart in the late nineteenth and early twentieth centuries. Churches of Christ then adopted a "modernist" stance in the sense that they increasingly bought into an optimistic, modern worldview and rejected the pessimistic, apocalyptic worldview of Stone and his successors, including David Lipscomb.

These three articles form a fascinating sequence. Hatch's article takes historical precedence as he examines the origins of the Stone-Campbell Movement in the early National period of US history. Harrell and Hughes, on the other hand, seek to define the emergence of Churches of Christ as a separate body at the end of the nineteenth century. The three essays complement each other chronologically, stretching from the late eighteenth century through the early twentieth.

The contributions of these authors to the movement's growing self-understanding have been immense. This book will make their material more readily available to students and others interested in the development of this significant American religious movement. Furthermore, it will aid those who are part of the movement to reflect again on the factors that have shaped us and perhaps better understand why we are who we are and how we are being shaped presently, to the end of making informed and historically-conscious choices about our future. Read, learn, and enjoy!

Douglas A. Foster
Abilene Christian University
April, 2000

# The Christian Movement and the Demand for a Theology of the People

**Nathan 0. Hatch**

In 1776, John Adams posed the question that would preoccupy his generation of American citizens and their children. "It is certain, in theory," he said, "that the only moral foundation of government is, the consent of the people. But to what extent shall we carry this principle?" The Revolution brought an accent of reality to a new self-evident truth, the sovereignty of the people, which Edmund Morgan has recently described as a "political fiction." For the founding fathers the fiction of popular sovereignty held some resemblance to the facts, but they fully expected the governed and the governors to "join in a benign conspiracy to suspend disbelief" in the new fiction, in other words, to believe it rhetorically rather than literally. The people were not so kind, however, and the shrill and unending debate that characterized American history from Adams to Andrew Jackson concerned how seriously this fiction should be taken.[1]

A number of scholars have recently explored the dimensions of this cultural ferment over the meaning of

[1] Charles Francis Adams, ed., *The Works of John Adams, Second President of the United States* (10 vols., Boston, 1850-1856) IX, 375; Edmund S. Morgan, "The Great Political Fiction," *New York Review of Books,* XXV (March 9, 1978), 13-18.

freedom. In the wake of their own and the French Revolution, Americans witnessed the rapid growth of voluntary organizations and popular newspapers, the formation of organized political parties amid heated and increasingly popular political debate, the armed protest of unprotected economic groups, sharp attacks upon elite professions and upon slavery, and new ideas of citizenship and representation, of old age and women's identity.[2] Eugene Genovese has even argued that a revolutionary ideology of liberty and equality transformed the character of slave resistance in North America and in the Caribbean.[3] Lamenting the awakening to political consciousness of the common man, Harrison Gray Otis gave to a Harvard audience in 1836 his view of what had happened since the Revolution: "Everywhere the disposition is found among those who live in the valleys, to ask those who live on the hills, 'How came we here and you there?' accompanied with intelligible demonstrations of a purpose in the former, to partake of the benefits of the mountain air."[4]

What became of American religion in these years—roughly 1780 to 1820—when traditional values were being turned upside down by what Gordon S. Wood has called a

---

[2] James A. Henretta, *The Evolution of American Society, 1700-1815* (Lexington, Mass., 1973); Richard D. Brown, *Modernization: The Transformation of American Life, 1600-1865* (New York, 1976); Richard D. Brown, "The Emergence of Voluntary Associations in Massachusetts, 1760-1830," *Journal of Voluntary Action Research*, II (April 1973), 64-73; Jackson Turner Main, "Government by the People: The American Revolution and the Democratization of the Legislatures," *William and Mary Quarterly*, XXIII (July 1966), 391-407; Bernard Bailyn, *The Ideological Origins of the American Revolution* (Cambridge, 1967); Richard E. Ellis, *The Jeffersonian Crisis: Courts and Politics in the Young Republic* (New York, 1971); David Brion Davis, *The Problem of Slavery in the Age of Revolution, 1770-1823* (Ithaca, 1975); David Hackett Fischer, *Growing Old in America* (New York, 1977); Robert A. Gross, *The Minutemen and Their World* (New York, 1976); and Mary Beth Norton, *The Revolutionary Experience of American Women, 1750-1800* (Boston, 1980).

[3] Eugene D. Genovese, *From Rebellion to Revolution: Afro-American Slave Revolts in the Making of the Modern World* (Baton Rouge, 1979).

[4] Harrison Gray Otis, who had delivered the English oration at Harvard when he graduated in 1783, was asked to give the primary address at Harvard's bicentennial celebration in 1836. His speech is the lament of an old man who had witnessed the "fiery furnace of democracy" destroy much of what he held dear. While he had hoped that the Revolution had been "completed by the establishment of independence," he lived to see a "new school" take charge that "would identify revolution with perpetual motion. They would put all ancient institutions, laws, customs, courts, colleges, and schools upon wheels, and keep them whirling for ever with the steam of their own eloquence." Josiah Quincy, *The History of Harvard University* (2 vols., Cambridge, 1840), II, 662-70.

"democratization of mind"?[5] Despite a wealth of recent scholarship on the role of religion in the coming of the American Revolution, surprisingly little work has been done on the changing nature of popular religion after the Revolution. This imbalance stems in part from the conventional division between the era of the republic's founding and that of the middle period, but it also reflects the simple fact that a quickened interest in religion as a cultural force has emerged within a broader historiographical tendency to downplay the social impact of the Revolution. The result has been that while historians have noted many links between the Great Awakening and the Revolution, they have not followed through to ask how rapid social change in the young republic affected structures of religious belief and organization.[6] What happened when people began to call for a strenuous application of popular sovereignty to the church? What did Christian freedom come to mean for people ready to question any source of authority that did not begin with an act of individual choice?

To explore these questions, this essay will focus on the cultural roots of a movement that assumed the name "Christian" or "Disciples of Christ." Between 1790 and 1815 this loose network of religious radicals demanded, in light of the American and French revolutions, a new dispensation set

---

[5] Gordon S. Wood, "The Democratization of Mind in the American Revolution," *Leadership in the American Revolution* (Washington, 1974), 63-89; and Gordon S. Wood, "Social Radicalism and Equality in the American Revolution," *The B. K. Smith Lectures in History* (Houston, 1976), 5-14.

[6] On the new scholarly interest in religion, see Henry F. May, "The Recovery of American Religious History," *American Historical Review,* LXX (Oct. 1964), 79-92. The broader trend to dismiss the social repercussions of the Revolution is evident in Frederick B. Tolles, "The American Revolution Considered as a Social Movement: A Re-Evaluation," *American Historical Review,* LX (Oct. 1954), 1-12. Studies of the Second Great Awakening in New England and the Great Revival in the Southwest have generally not addressed the question of how cultural ferment might have altered religion; they have focused, rather, on how traditional religion championed the revival technique in order to impose social order upon a disordered and secularized society. See Perry Miller, "From Covenant to Revival," in *The Shaping of American Religion,* ed. J. W. Smith and A. L. Jamison (Princeton, 1961), 350; Lois W. Banner, "Religious Benevolence as Social Control: A Critique of an Interpretation," *Journal of American History,* LX (June 1973), 23-41; and John B. Boles, *The Great Revival, 1787-1805: The Origins of the Southern Evangelical Mind* (Lexington, Ky., 1972). More sensitive to the ongoing impact of the Revolution in religious affairs is Donald G. Mathews, "The Second Great Awakening as an Organizing Process, 1780-1830: An Hypothesis," *American Quarterly,* XXI (Spring 1969), 23-43.

free from the trammels of history, a new kind of institutional church premised on the self-evident principles of republicanism, and a new form of biblical authority calling for the inalienable right of common people to interpret the New Testament for themselves. The central figures in the reform movement—Elias Smith in New England, James O'Kelly in Virginia, Barton Stone in Kentucky, and Alexander Campbell in Pennsylvania—were a motley crew with few common characteristics, but they all moved independently to similar conclusions within a fifteen-year span. A Calvinist Baptist, a Methodist, and two Presbyterians all found traditional sources of authority anachronistic and found themselves groping toward similar definitions of egalitarian religion.[7] In a culture that increasingly balked at vested interests, symbols of hierarchy, and timeless authorities, a remarkable number of people would wake up one morning to find it self-evident that the priesthood of all believers meant just that—religion of, by, and for the people.

At the dawn of the nineteenth century, the Federalist citadel of Essex County, Massachusetts, witnessed a major assault on its well-bred and high-toned culture. Religious enthusiasm had taken hold among common people and its rude challenge to authority dismayed even the tolerant Jeffersonian diarist William Bentley of Salem. As late as 1803, Bentley had confided smugly that Essex County remained virtually free of sects. During the next five years, he watched with dismay the lower orders of his community championing "religious convulsions," "domestic fanaticism," and "Meeting-Mania." In chronicling the parade of sects that won attention—Baptist, Freewill Baptist, Methodist, Universalist, and Christian—Bentley noted the first field

[7] Luther P. Gerlach and Virginia H. Hine define a social "movement" as "a group of people who are organized for, ideologically motivated by, and committed to a purpose which implements some form of personal or social change; who are actively engaged in the recruitment of others; and whose influence is spreading in opposition to the established order within which it originated." Luther P. Gerlach and Virginia H. Hine, *People, Power, Change: Movements of Social Transformation* (Indianapolis, 1970), xvi. The Christians, like the movements of which Gerlach and Hine speak, were decentralized and segmented, their web-like structures without clear lines of authority and often dependent upon shared publications. Their unity stemmed from little more than common ideology and perceived opposition from religious and political elites.

meeting in the county since George Whitefield, preaching by blacks and illiterate sailors, and servants angering their employers by frequenting night lectures "as in Mother Hutchinson's time." What Bentley found most appalling was that "the rabble" not only noised abroad strange doctrine but actually went beyond what they were told, attempting "to explain, condemn and reveal" religious matters. The people, he groaned, were doing theology for themselves.[8]

Bentley saved his sharpest barbs for an itinerant preacher, the "notorious" Smith who regularly barnstormed through Essex County, preaching in the open air, singing in the streets, and accosting people to question their spiritual state. If this was not enough to discomfit the respectable citizens of Salem, Smith kept the pot boiling by leaving behind bundles of his tracts and pamphlets.[9]

For all its parallels with the dissent of a Whitefield or an Isaac Backus, Smith's gospel for the people did have one different twist. It was laced with the language of politics and reflected the experience of a man whose radical pilgrimage began with a political conversion. Until 1800 Smith filled the pulpit of the respectable Baptist Church in Woburn, Massachusetts, and gave little attention to political questions of the day. During the election of 1800, however, he fell under the influence of the radical Jeffersonian publicist Benjamin Austin, Jr., who wrote regularly for the *Boston Independent Chronicle*. Smith quickly imbibed Austin's heady wine, which made much of the right of common people to think and act for themselves. Resigning from his church—as a manifesto of his own liberty—and denouncing formal religion of every kind, Smith began to translate the sovereignty of the people to the sphere of religion.[10] "Let us be republicans indeed," he declared in 1809. "Many are *republicans* as to *government,* and yet are but half

[8] William Bentley, *The Diary of William Bentley, D. D.* (4 vols., Salem, Mass., 1911), III, 65, 503, 515, 271.

[9] In May 1805 William Bentley commented about Elias Smith that "the press has lately vomited out many nauseous things from this writer." *Ibid.*, 157, 370, 291.

[10] Elias Smith, *The Life, Conversion, Preaching, Travels and Sufferings of Elias Smith* (Portsmouth, N.H., 1816), 341-42.

republicans, being in matters of religion still bound to a catechism, creed, covenant or superstitious priest. Venture to be as independent in things of religion, as those which respect the government in which you live."[11] From Portsmouth, New Hampshire, Smith launched the first religious newspaper in the United States, a fortnightly *Herald of Gospel Liberty,* which he edited from 1808 to 1818. From that forum and in scores of pamphlets and sermons, he and a band of fifty or so itinerants, who called themselves merely Christians, carried on a blistering attack upon Baptists, Congregationalists, Methodists, and Federalists of any religious persuasion. The *Herald of Gospel Liberty,* which by 1815 had fourteen hundred subscribers and over fifty agents around the country, became a vehicle of communication for other individuals who were moving independently to the same conclusion as Smith.[12]

From Virginia came word of O'Kelly's Republican Methodists, founded in 1794 to undo the "ecclesiastical monarchy" in the Methodist church. A prime mover among early Virginia Methodists, O'Kelly could not abide the bishopric of Francis Asbury and withdrew with over thirty ministers to form a connection which had as many as twenty thousand members when it merged with Smith's forces, under

[11] Elias Smith, *The Lovingkindness of God Displayed in the Triumph of Republicanism in America: Being a Discourse Delivered at Taunton (Mass.) July Fourth, 1809; at the Celebration of American Independence* (n.p., 1809), 32. Smith's colleague Abner Jones also experienced what he called a "disintegration" of his Calvinist beliefs and was quick to note the theological implications of demands for social equality. "In giving the reader an account of my birth and parentage," Jones wrote in 1807, "I shall not (like the celebrated Franklin and others,) strive to prove that I arose from a family of eminence; believing that all men are born equal, and that every man shall die for his own iniquity." Abner Jones, *Memoirs of the Life and Experience, Travels and Preaching of Abner Jones* (Exeter, N.H., 1807), 3.

[12] For a brief sketch of Smith's life, see William G. McLoughlin, *New England Dissent, 1630-1883: The Baptists and the Separation of Church and State* (2 vols., Cambridge, 1971), II, 745-49. Otherwise, no one has undertaken a serious study of Smith, despite his prominence as a religious and political radical in New England from 1800 to 1820, his scores of publications addressed to a popular audience, his newspaper that ran for a decade, and his fascinating memoir. The number of his itinerant followers is taken from one of his Congregational assailants. Thomas Andros, *The Scriptures Liable to be Wrested to Men's Own Destruction, and an Instance of This Found, in the Writings of Elias Smith* (Taunton, Mass., 1817), 18. A list of agents for Smith's newspaper is found in *Herald of Gospel Liberty,* Aug. 18, 1809, p. 104. For the number of subscribers, see *ibid.,* Sept. 29, 1815, p. 720. On Smith's movement, which became known as the Christian Connection, see Thomas H. Olbricht, "Christian Connection and Unitarian Relations," *Restoration Quarterly,* IX (Sept. 1966), 160-86.

the name Christian, in 1809.[13] "Episcopacy makes a bad appearance in our republican world," O'Kelly argued in 1798. "Francis was born and nurtured in the land of Bishops and Kings and what is bred in the bone, is hard to get out of the flesh."[14] O'Kelly, who had taken up arms in the Revolution and served a brief stint as a British captive, argued that he was "too sensible of the sweets of liberty, to be content any longer under British chains.... As a son of America, and a Christian," he challenged Asbury, "I shall oppose your political measures and contend for the Saviour's government. I contend for Bible government, Christian equality, and the Christian name."[15]

Stone was an equally interesting figure who had ventured upon much the same pilgrimage prior to the appearance of the *Herald of Gospel Liberty.* In 1802, in the wake of the Cane Ridge Revival in Kentucky, Stone decided he could no longer live under Presbyterian doctrine or church organization. A year later, he and five other ministers pushed this idea to its logical extreme and proclaimed that it was not just the Presbyterians who were wrong: all church structures were suspect. Signing "The Last Will and Testament of Springfield Presbytery," these men vowed to follow nothing but the Christian name and the New Testament.[16]

Scholars have generally viewed Stone's beliefs as the product of the rough-and-tumble context of the frontier and of

---

[13] The best treatment of James O'Kelly is Charles Franklin Kilgore, *The James O'Kelly Schism in the Methodist Episcopal Church* (Mexico City, 1963). See also Edward J. Drinkhouse, *History of Methodist Reform* (2 vols., Baltimore, 1899), I; and Milo T. Morrill, *A History of the Christian Denomination in America* (Dayton, 1912). O'Kelly's primary works are James O'Kelly, *The Author's Apology for Protesting against the Methodist Episcopal Government* (Richmond, 1798); and James O'Kelly, *A Vindication of the Author's Apology* (Raleigh, 1801).

[14] O'Kelly, *Author's Apology,* 4, 21.

[15] O'Kelly, *Vindication,* 60-61.

[16] "The Last Will and Testament of Springfield Presbytery," in John Rogers, *The Biography of Elder B. Warren Stone* (New York, 1972), 51-53. For other primary accounts of this movement, see Barton W. Stone, *An Apology for Renouncing the Jurisdiction of the Synod of Kentucky* (Lexington, Ky., 1804); [Richard McNemar], *Observations on Church Government, by the Presbytery of Springfield* (Cincinnati, 1807); Robert Marshall and James Thompson, *A Brief Historical Account of Sundry Things in the Doctrines and State of the Christian, or, as It Is Commonly Called, the Newlight Church* (Cincinnati, 1811); Levi Purviance, *The Biography of Elder David Purviance* (Dayton, 1848); and Robert H. Bishop, *An Outline of the History of the Church in the State of Kentucky, during a Period of Forty Years: Containing the Memoirs of Rev. David Rice* (Lexington, Ky., 1824).

the rampant emotionalism of the Great Revival.[17] Stone was a rawboned character, no doubt, but he also spent his formative years during the Revolution, and his theology of "gospel-liberty" reflected this early experience. "From my earliest recollection I drank deeply into the spirit of liberty," he confessed late in life, "and was so warmed by the soul-inspiring draughts, that I could not hear the name of British, or tories, without feeling a rush of blood through the whole system. . . . I confess their magic influence to this advanced day of my life." It was not without deep connotation that Stone characterized his break with the Presbyterians as the "declaration of our independence."[18]

The final member of the quartet whose democratic theology this essay analyzes is the Scottish immigrant Alexander Campbell—the only college graduate among the four and the only one not to participate in the American Revolution.[19] Whatever Alexander Campbell may have brought to America of his Scottish and Presbyterian heritage, he found much of it convenient to discard for an explicitly American theology. Writing to his uncle back in Scotland in 1815, he described his seven years in the United States: "During this period of years my mind and circumstances have undergone many revolutions . . . I have . . . renounced much of the traditions and errors of my early education." He described the change elsewhere in these words: "My mind was, for a time, set loose from all its former moorings. It was not a simple change: but a new commencement. . . . the whole landscape of Christianity presented itself to my mind in a new

[17] There is a considerable body of uncritical denominational literature on Barton W. Stone by the Disciples of Christ. See William Garrett West, *Barton Warren Stone: Early American Advocate of Christian Unity* (Nashville, 1954). For emphasis on Stone's contribution to the revivalist heritage of the South, see Boles, *Great Revival.* For appreciation of Stone in his full cultural context, see Ralph Morrow, "The Great Revival, the West, and the Crisis of the Church," in *The Frontier Re-examined,* ed. John F. McDermott (Urbana, 1967), 65-78.

[18] Rogers, *Biography of Elder B. Warren Stone,* 3, 47.

[19] For discussions of the origins of the Campbellites, see David Edwin Harrell, Jr., *Quest for a Christian America: The Disciples of Christ and American Society to 1866* (Nashville, 1966); Robert Frederick West, *Alexander Campbell and Natural Religion* (New Haven, 1948); Lester G. McAllister, *Thomas Campbell: Man of the Book* (St. Louis, 1954); and Errett Gates, *The Early Relation and Separation of Baptists and Disciples* (Chicago, 1904). In addition, see the extensive memoirs of father and son: Alexander Campbell, *Memoirs of Elder Thomas Campbell* (Cincinnati, 1861); and Robert Richardson, *Memoirs of Alexander Campbell* (2 vols., Cincinnati, 1913).

attitude and position."[20] By 1830 Alexander Campbell's quest for primitive Christianity led his movement, the Disciples of Christ, into union with Stone's Christians. By 1860 their denomination claimed about 200,000 adherents, the fifth largest Protestant body in the United States.[21] More important, for our purposes, his theology fell into an unmistakable pattern that was emerging in the early republic. Smith, O'Kelly, and Stone all knew what Campbell meant when he proclaimed that July 4, 1776, was "a day to be remembered as was the Jewish Passover. . . . This revolution, taken in all its influences, will make men free indeed."[22]

In many ways the message of the Christians built upon the kind of radical piety that Americans had known since the Great Awakening of the 1740s. These new reformers hammered relentlessly at the simple themes of sin, grace, and conversion; they organized fellowships that resisted social distinctions and welcomed spontaneous experience; and they denounced any religion that smacked of being bookish, cold, and formal. What sets the Christians apart from earlier revivalists is the extent to which they wrestled self-consciously with the loss of traditional sources of authority and found in democratic political culture a cornerstone for new foundations. Taking seriously the mandate of liberty and equality, the Christians espoused reform in three areas. First, they called for a revolution within the church that would place laity and clergy on an equal footing and would exalt the conscience of the individual over the collective will of any congregation or church organization. Second, they rejected the traditions of learned theology altogether and called for a

---

20 Richardson, *Memoirs of Alexander Campbell*, I, 465-66, 438. Many scholars have assumed that Thomas and Alexander Campbell applied to an American context beliefs that they had learned under the influence of Scottish reformers such as Robert Haldane and James Alexander Haldane. See, for example, Sydney E. Ahlstrom, *A Religious History of the American People* (New Haven, 1972), 448-49. The early documents of the Campbellite movement, however, manifest a keen awareness that the issues to be faced were, in their intensity at least, peculiarly American and demanded new solutions. See, for example, Thomas Campbell, *The Declaration and Address of the Christian Association of Washington* (Washington, PA., 1809).

21 Lester G. McAllister and William E. Tucker, *Journey in Faith: A History of the Christian Church (Disciples of Christ)* (St. Louis, 1975), 154-55.

22 Alexander Campbell, "An Oration in Honor of the Fourth of July, 1830," *Popular Lectures and Addresses* (Philadelphia, 1863), 374-75.

new view of history that welcomed inquiry and innovation. Finally, they called for a populist hermeneutic premised on the inalienable right of every person to understand the New Testament for themselves.

A zeal to dismantle mediating elites within the church, more than anything else, triggered the Christians' revolt against tradition. O'Kelly broke with Asbury when the Methodist bishop refused to put up with representative government in the church. Smith bade farewell to Backus and the Warren Association after influential colleagues criticized his plain dress and suggested that the respectable parishioners of Woburn, Massachusetts deserved more decorum. Both Stone and Thomas Campbell—Alexander's father, who had preceded him to America—withdrew from the Presbyterians when their orthodox colleagues began to clamp down on their freedom of inquiry concerning Presbyterian standards. Before their respective separations, each of these men in his own way had offered stern opposition to received tradition; yet their dissent was contained within taken-for-granted cultural boundaries. Once they had severed organizational ties, however, mild questions reappeared as seething hostility, and suggestions for reform turned to ecclesiastical defiance.

The Christians excelled at popular communication. They ferreted out converts with an unremitting itinerancy and cranked out an avalanche of pamphlet and newspaper copy, which, in its form and content, conspired against social distinction.[23] Smith was aware of his innovative role when he began the first religious newspaper in the United States; he confessed on its opening page that the utility of such a paper had been suggested to him by the explosion of popular print all around. "In a short and cheap way," he asserted, "a general knowledge of our affairs is diffused through the whole." While his paper did include accounts of revivals of religion throughout the world, its overall strategy showed little resemblance to previous revival periodicals such as the *Christian History* of the Great Awakening, largely an intramural communication among the clergy. By promoting

---

[23] "Elias Smith was here last week, distributing his books & pamphlets, & preached a lecture last week without sparing any of the hirelings as he calls them." Bentley, *Diary,* III, 388.

in common language the idea that *"right is equal among all,"* Smith knew that he would incur the judgment that he was "stirring up the people to revolt" and "turning the world upside down."[24] Just as he expected, the established clergy found his "vulgar stories and malicious sarcasm" totally beneath them, but they could hardly ignore the popularity of his "poisoned arrows of ridicule and reproach."[25]

The style of Smith's communication is well illustrated in one of his early pamphlets, *The Clergyman's Looking-Glass,* a stinging attack on men of the cloth that went through at least a dozen printings. Smith juxtaposed passages of the New Testament with satirical jibes at the contemporary clergy in mock-scripture style. After quoting from 1 Peter the instructions that elders were to serve God's flock "not for filthy lucre . . . neither as being lords over God's heritage," Smith gave his Petrine rendition of the modern clergy:

> The reverend clergy who are with me I advise, who am also a clergyman, and a D. D., a member of that respectable body, who are numerous, and 'who seek honor one of another;' and a partaker of the benefit of it; feed yourselves upon the church and parish, over which we have settled you for life, and who are obliged to support you, whether they like you or not; taking the command by constraint, for filthy lucre, not of a ready mind, as lords over men's souls, not as ensamples to them, and when commencement day shall appear, you shall receive some honorary title, which shall make you appear very respectable among the reverend clergy.[26]

---

24 *Herald of Gospel Liberty*, Sept. 1, 1808, p. 1.

25 Stephen Porter, a Presbyterian clergyman, attempted to ward off the influence of Smith and his lieutenants among his congregation. Stephen Porter, *A Discourse, in Two Parts, Addressed to the Presbyterian Congregation in Ballston* (Ballston Spa, N.Y., 1814), 42-44.

26 Elias Smith, *The Clergyman's Looking-Glass: Being a History of the Birth, Life, and Death of Anti-Christ* (Portsmouth, N.H., 1803), 11. For examples of Smith's sensitivity to elitist codes of all sorts, even while he was still a Baptist, see Smith, *Life*, 279-80.

In a similar vein, Alexander Campbell used his first newspaper, the *Christian Baptist,* to mock the pretensions of the clergy. In a burlesque "Third Epistle of Peter," a document reportedly discovered by a monk, he instructed preachers to live well, wear the best clothes, adorn themselves with high-sounding titles, drink costly wine, and fleece the people.[27] Evangelicals in the past had often questioned the spiritual state of individual clergymen; the Christians now took the liberty to slander the entire profession as money-grubbing tyrants.

This kind of billingsgate journalism employed two very powerful appeals. In the first place, it portrayed society as horizontally polarized: the people were arrayed against elites of all kind, military, legal, civic, and religious. In an early edition of the *Herald of Gospel Liberty,* Smith sketched a most revealing dialogue between the people and the privileged class. "The picture, is this: two companies standing in sight of each other, one large, the other small. The large containing every profession useful to society, the other small, wearing marks of distinction, appearing as though they did no labour, yet in rich attire, glittering with gold and silver, while their plump and ruddy countenances, prove them persons of leisure and riches." Seething with resentment, the people of Smith's dialogue happened to overhear what the privileged were saying to each other: "To mix and place ourselves on a level with the *common people,* would be beyond all measure degrading and vilifying. What! are they not born to serve us? and are we not men of a totally distinct blood and superior pedigree?" In response, the people insisted that they were going "to take the management of our affairs into our own hands.... When the people declare themselves free, such *privileged classes* will be as useles[s] as candles at noonday."[28]

Abel M. Sargent, another radical figure associated with the Christians, used his paper, the *Halcyon Itinerary and True Millennium Messenger*, to present a virtual class analysis of society. Writing in 1807 to extol Thomas Jefferson as the

[27] *Christian Baptist*, July 4, 1823, p. 280.

[28] *Herald of Gospel Liberty*, Dec. 8, 1808, pp. 29-30.

forerunner of a new millennial age, Sargent demanded that life, liberty, and happiness be extended to "the oppressed who have been deprived of them." His images of society bristle with the ongoing conflict between the powerful and the oppressed: "How often do we see it the case in earthly courts, under the dominion of the beast, that the power and influence of money and false Agency over-balance equity and right; so that the poor have but a dull chance to obtain Justice in carnal courts; and again, how often is the poor industrious and honest labourer, reduced to the absolute necessity of yielding up his rights and falling a prey to cruelty and injustice, merely for want of money enough to discharge the fees of those whose interest and livings (like the wolf and raven) depend on the ruin and destruction of others."[29]

For all its innovation, however, this bombast against the privileged also employed a second appeal. It appropriated the rhetoric of civil and religious liberty that the respectable clergy had made popular during the Revolution and marshaled it for an entirely new purpose, to topple its very architects. The Christians exploited to the hilt the potent themes of tyranny, slavery, and Antichrist; they delighted in regaling their audiences with the latest chapter in the saga of the beast and the whore of Babylon. Simply put, Antichrist now worked his evil machinations through elites of all kind, particularly the clergy. In a splendid example of the multivalency of language, rhetoric that had seemed benign when used by respectable clergymen during the Revolution came to have radical connotations when abstracted from a restricted context and transferred to people who had reason to

[29] Abel M. Sargent founded a radical sect in Marietta, Ohio, where he published six issues of *Halcyon Itinerary and True Millennium Messenger*. The quotation is found in *Halcyon Itinerary and True Millennium Messenger* (Dec. 1807), 147-48. For a letter from Sargent to Smith, see *Herald of Gospel Liberty*, Aug. 16, 1811, 310. On Sargent, see John W. Simpson, *A Century of Church Life* (Marietta, 1896), 31.

lash out at vested interests.[30]

But what end did the Christians have in view when decrying ecclesiastical authority? What positive implications did they wring out of the notion of religious liberty? Smith came right to the point in an early issue of the *Herald of Gospel Liberty* when he contrasted the mere separation of church and state with "being wholly free to examine for ourselves, what is truth." He argued that every last Christian had the "unalienable right" to follow "the scripture wherever it leads him, even an equal right with the Bishops and Pastors of the churches . . . even though his principles may, in many things, be contrary to what the Reverend D. D.'s call Orthodoxy."[31] Using the same language, Alexander Campbell pressed for "the inalienable right of all laymen to examine the sacred writings for themselves." Brimming with conspiratorial notions of how clergymen of every stripe had "hoodwinked" the people, this logic eventually led each of these Christian leaders to demand that the traditional distinction between clergy and laity be abolished and that any leadership in the local church function according to new rules: "Liberty is nowhere safe in any hands excepting those of the people themselves."[32] With demands for this sort of liberation afoot, it is little wonder that Congregational and Presbyterian clergymen came to view the Christians as but another tentacle of the Bavarian Illuminati's conspiracy to

[30] Christians assailed the clergy as "tyrannical oppressors," "the mystery of iniquity," "friends of monarchy religion," "old tories," "an *aristocratical body of uniform nobility*," and "hireling priests"; people who would submit to such tyrants they labeled priest-ridden, slavishly dependent, passively obedient. See Smith, *Life*, 384, 402-03; *Herald of Gospel Liberty*, Oct. 13, 1809, p. 117; O'Kelly, *Vindication*, 47. In 1815 Smith claimed that most people in New England from forty to seventy years old could remember the respectable clergy emphasizing apocalyptic themes such as "*Anti-Christ, mystery Babylon*, the *great whore* that sitteth on many waters, the *beast* with seven heads and ten horns, the *man of sin* &c." *Herald of Gospel Liberty*, May 20, 1815, p. 685. On the multivalency of language, see J. G. A. Pocock, *Politics, Language and Time: Essays on Political Thought and History* (New York, 1971), 3-41; and Harry S. Stout, "Religion, Communications, and the Ideological Origins of the American Revolution," *William and Mary Quarterly*, XXXIV (Oct. 1977), 538.

[31] Smith, *Lovingkindness of God Displayed*, 26-27; Smith, *Life*, 352-53. See also *Herald of Gospel Liberty*, April 14, 1809, p. 67.

[32] *Christian Baptist*, Jan. 2, 1826, p. 209; Smith, *Life*, 402-03; *Herald of Gospel Liberty*, Sept. 15, 1808, p. 6. See also Richardson, *Memoirs of Alexander Campbell*, I, 382-83.

overthrow authority in church and state.[33]

The Christian idea of religious liberty stands in marked contrast to the eighteenth-century notion that religious liberty meant the civil right to choose or not to choose affiliation with a church. The religious dissent that had come out of the Great Awakening, despite its popular sources, had never begun to suggest that power should be surrendered to the people in this fashion. The Baptists in Virginia set themselves off from the culture of gentlemen by striving for more order, more discipline, and more social control within the local congregation.[34] In New England, as well, Baptists and Separatists called for closed communion and a tighter discipline within the pure church. By the 1760s, they were educating their clergy, forming associations to regulate doctrine and local disputes, and, as their people began to drift away to other sects during the Revolution, actually imposing stiff creedal tests upon local churches. Backus did not long for some new order that leveled the clergy and exalted the laity; he reminisced, instead, about the pious fathers of early New England. He argued time and again that his Baptists agreed "with the most eminent fathers of New England, except in sprinkling infants upon the faith of their parents and calling it baptism."[35] The same point has been made about the Separatists of New England: "they were reformers, not rebels; . . . they wished to fulfill their history as Puritans, not repudiate it."[36]

In contrast, the Christians called for the abolition of organizational restraints of any kind. In the "Last Will and

---

33 See David Rice, *An Epistle to the Citizens of Kentucky, Professing Christianity* (Lexington, Ky., 1805), 11-12.

34 Rhys Isaac, "Evangelical Revolt: The Nature of the Baptists' Challenge to the Traditional Order in Virginia, 1765 to 1775," *William and Mary Quarterly*, XXXI (July 1974), 345-68.

35 Isaac Backus, *A History of New England with Particular Reference to the Denomination of Christians Called Baptists* (2 vols., Newton, Mass., 1871), II, 487. For evidence of the Baptist quest for respectability in the generation after the Great Awakening, see C. C. Goen, *Revivalism and Separatism in New England, 1740-1800* (New Haven, Conn., 1962). For the reaction of Baptists to the dissent spawned by the Revolution, see McLoughlin, *New England Dissent*, II, 710.

36 James Patrick Walsh, "The Pure Church in Eighteenth Century Connecticut" (Ph.D. diss., Columbia University, 1964), 143.

Testament of Springfield Presbytery," Stone and five colleagues dissolved their association, already a splinter group from the Presbyterian church. Only by renouncing all institutional forms could "the oppressed . . . go free, and taste the sweets of gospel liberty."[37] Alexander Campbell did not even want to hear the words "church government": "We have no system of our own, or of others, to substitute in lieu of the reigning systems. We only aim at substituting the New Testament."[38] In a similar vein, Stone and his associates declared that the attempt "to impose any form of government upon the church . . . should be justly abandoned by every child of gospel liberty." They went on to say that any human form of government would be "like binding two or more dead bodies together" and coercing people "like parts of a machine."[39] The organization of Protestant churches, which in colonial culture had been seen as vibrant and alive—the very body of Christ—now smacked of being dead and mechanistic.

By their appeal to "Bible government," the Christians removed the issue of power and authority from any concrete application. They opposed all ecclesiastical names not found in the New Testament, advocated the right of the individual unilaterally to withdraw from church membership, and refused to adhere to creeds as tests of fellowship, to undergo theological examinations, or to offer a confession of faith upon joining a church. In short, no human organization could exist that did not spring from the uncoerced will of the individual. When pressed by Bishop Asbury to heed the scriptural injunction, "Obey them that have rule over you," O'Kelly responded: "Rule over, is no more than for the church to follow those guides who delivered unto them the Word of God." O'Kelly was suggesting that, by submitting to the New Testament, a Christian in 1800 never would have to

---

[37] Rogers, *Biography of Elder B. Warren Stone*, 51-53.

[38] *Christian Baptist*, Nov. 3, 1823, p. 25; Richardson, *Memoirs of Alexander Campbell*, II, 63-64.

[39] [McNemar], *Observations on Church Government*, 4, 9, 15. This pamphlet, the best-developed statement of Christian ecclesiology, rejects "external rules" and insists that all human organization spring from the deliberate and uncoerced choice of the individual.

doff his hat to any mere mortal.[40]

In a passing reference in *The American Revolution Considered as a Social Movement,* J. Franklin Jameson noted the growth in numbers and zeal of those religious bodies that were revolting against Calvinism—the Methodists, Universalists, Unitarians, and Freewill Baptists.[41] He might also have included the loose combination of mavericks who called themselves merely Christians. Except for O'Kelly, whose Methodist background made Calvinism a dead issue, the other primary figures in this movement—Smith, Stone, and Campbell—were all zealous Calvinists early in life and experienced a conversion to what they called gospel liberty.

On one level this revolt seems simple enough to understand. The heady concepts of liberty that had led to denunciations of institutional constraints also rendered meaningless such concepts as unconditional election and limited atonement. After great intellectual turmoil, each of these men came to the point of harmonizing theology with their social experience. As a Calvinist, Stone confessed that he was "embarrassed with many abstruse doctrines." "Scores of objections would continually roll across my mind." What he called the "labyrinth of Calvinism" left his mind "distressed," "perplexed," and "bewildered." He found relief from this dissonance of values only as he came to attack Calvinism as falsehood.[42]

The revolt against Calvinism, however, becomes somewhat harder to understand when placed in its full context. The Christians were venting their hostility not against Calvinism in some narrow sense, as if they might find their niche as Methodists or Freewill Baptists, but against an entire system. "We are not personally acquainted with the writings of John Calvin," wrote Robert Marshall and John

---

[40] O'Kelly, *Vindication*, 49. For similar expressions of resistance to human mediation of divine authority by Alexander Campbell and Thomas Campbell, see *Christian Baptist*, April 3, 1826, p. 229, and Campbell, *Declaration and Address of the Christian Association*, 3. For the recurrence of this line of thought a generation later, see Lewis Perry, *Radical Abolitionism: Anarchy and the Government of God in Antislavery Thought* (Ithaca, 1973).

[41] J. Franklin Jameson, *The American Revolution Considered as a Social Movement* (Princeton, 1926), 157.

[42] Rogers, *Biography of Elder B. Warren Stone,* 14, 31, 33.

Thompson, two of Stone's colleagues, "nor are we certain how nearly we agree with his views of divine truth; neither do we care."[43]

This was no mere revolt against Calvinism but against theology itself. What was going on that gave Stone the audacity not only to reject the doctrine of the Trinity—Unitarians right and left were doing that—but also to maintain, "I have not spent, perhaps, an hour in ten years in thinking about the Trinity"? What made it credible for Smith, after seriously debating whether he would be a Calvinist or a Universalist, to remove the dilemma altogether by dropping them both? "I was now without a system," he confessed with obvious relief, "and felt ready to search the scriptures."[44] How could these men convince themselves, not to mention their followers, that the stage was set for a church without organization and a theology without theory?

Whatever else the Christians demanded, the rallying cry of their theological revolution was a new view of history. They called for a new dispensation of gospel liberty, radically discontinuous with the past. They advocated new theological ground rules that dismissed everything since the New Testament as irrelevant, if not destructive. What led Americans in the finest evangelical tradition of Jonathan Edwards, John Witherspoon, Backus, and Asbury to repudiate their heritage? Furthermore, what gave credence to the idea that they were standing on the brink of a new age?

One cannot understand the Christians apart from their deep conviction that they had witnessed in the American and French revolutions the most momentous historical events in two millennia—a *novus ordo seclorum*. The opening line of the *Herald of Gospel Liberty* proclaimed that "the age in which we live may certainly be distinguished from others in the history of Man," and Smith was quick to point out that it was the struggle for liberty and the rights of mankind that set it apart. According to Smith, the foundations of Christ's

---

[43] Marshall and Thompson, *Brief Historical Account*, 3-4.

[44] Elias Smith, *Sermons, Containing an Illustration of the Prophecies* (Exeter, N.H., 1808), vi.

millennial kingdom were laid in the American and French revolutions. "The time will come," he said, "when there will not be a *crowned head* on earth. Every attempt which is made to keep up a Kingly government, and to pull down a Republican one, will . . . serve to destroy monarchy. . . . Every small piece, or plan, of Monarchy which is a part of the *image* [of Antichrist] will be wholly dissolved, when *the people* are resolved to 'live free or die.'"[45]

The following year in Washington, Pennsylvania, Thomas Campbell published the first salvo of their movement and pointed to the same state of revolutionary and apocalyptic affairs: "Do ye not discern the signs of the times? Have not the two witnesses arisen from their state of political death, from under the long proscription of ages? . . . Who amongst us has not heard the report of these things—of these lightenings and thunderings, and voices, of this tremendous earthquake and great hail; of these awful convulsions and revolutions that have dashed and are dashing to pieces the nations like a potter's vessel?" In their view, such political convulsions spoke as the voice of providence "loudly and expressly calling us to repentance and reformation. . . . Resume that precious, that dear bought liberty, wherewith Christ has made his people free; a liberty from subjection to any authority but his own, in matters of religion. Call no man father. . . ." Alexander Campbell argued that the War for Independence unveiled a new epoch that would deliver men from "the melancholy thraldom of relentless systems." America's "political regeneration" gave her the responsibility to lead a comparable "ecclesiastical renovation."[46] An expectancy and overt respect for novelty characterized the Christians, as Stone's two associates confessed: "We confidently thought that the Millennium was just at hand, and

---

[45] *Herald of Gospel Liberty,* Sept. 1, 1808, p. 1; Elias Smith, *A Discourse Delivered at Jefferson Hall, Thanksgiving Day, November 25, 1802; and Redelivered (by Request) the Wednesday Evening Following, at the Same Place: The Subject, Nebuchadnezzar's Dream* (Portsmouth, N.H., 1803), 30-32. The sociologist Guy E. Swanson has argued that the political forms under which a people live significantly color their theological perceptions, particularly in times of rapid change. See Guy E. Swanson, *Religion and Regime: A Sociological Account of the Reformation* (Ann Arbor, 1967), 231.

[46] Campbell, *Declaration and Address of the Christian Association,* 14; Campbell, "Oration in Honor of the Fourth of July," 374; *Christian Baptist,* Feb. 6, 1826, p. 213.

that a glorious church would soon be formed; we thought, also, that we had found the very plan for its formation and growth." Opponents of these men agreed, moreover, that a sense of apocalyptic urgency had fueled the movement from the start.[47]

If the age of democratic revolutions gave the Christians good reason to sever ties with the past, it also suggested egalitarian models for a new age. In describing the true gospel that would revolutionize the world, Alexander Campbell called it "the declaration of independence of the kingdom of Jesus." Smith and Stone chose the same term to describe their withdrawal from the Baptists and Presbyterians, respectively. Similarly, O'Kelly claimed that he broke with the Methodists because they left him no option but "unlimited submission" or separation.[48] The lengths to which they allowed political idioms to color their thinking are sometimes difficult to comprehend: for example, they referred to the early church as a republican society with a New Testament constitution. In 1807, however, one maverick Christian in Marietta, Ohio, outdid them all, claiming that "the great potentate of the world, in principle, is the most *genuine* REPUBLICAN that ever existed."[49]

From a modern viewpoint, it may seem odd that men so committed to the separation of church and state held up a given political structure as a model for the church. They endowed the republic with the same divine authority as did defenders of the Standing Order such as Timothy Dwight and Noah Webster, but for opposite reasons. The republic became a new city on a hill not because it kept faith with Puritan tradition, but because it sounded the death knell for corporate and hierarchic conceptions of the social order. For these radical sectarians, the constitutional guarantees of separation of church and state laid the groundwork for a new age. In

[47] Marshall and Thompson, *Brief Historical Account*, 255. Presbyterian David Rice complained in 1805 about Stone and his followers: "Another thing that prepared the minds of many for the reception of error, was their high expectation of the speedy approach of the Millennium." Rice, *Epistle to the Citizens of Kentucky*, 13.

[48] Campbell, "Oration in Honor of the Fourth of July," 377; Smith, *Life*, 292; Rogers, *Biography of Elder B. Warren Stone*, 47; O'Kelly, *Author's Apology*, 52.

[49] Abel Sargent, *Halcyon Itinerary and True Millennium Messenger*, V (Dec. 1807), 146.

sum, a government so enlightened as to tell the churches to go their own way must have also had prophetic power to tell them which way to go.[50]

Millennialism, then, served different functions for the Christians from those that it had during the Great Awakening. Revivals of the 1740s drew upon millennial themes to challenge traditionalists in the name of a greater commitment to traditional values.[51] This sense of eschatological drama, furthermore, served to define an evangelical identity over against political culture. By contrast, the democratic ferment experienced by the Christians convinced them that, in thinking about the future, they should work to erase the memory of the past and should learn from political culture whatever they could about a gospel of equality.

The Christians expressed their revolt against history most clearly in the radical way they chose to read the Bible. Amid unraveling cultural norms, they tenaciously clung to one final, unassailable authority, the *ipse dixit* of the New Testament. The direct propositions of Scripture became the only ground of certainty. In a letter to the *Herald of Gospel Liberty* in 1809, seventeen Christian ministers spelled out this central plank of the Christian platform: "In consequence of your receiving Christ as only head, and ruler of his church, it necessarily follows, *that his law as contained in the New Testament,* should be received without any addition, abridgment, alterations, or embellishments, to the exclusion of all articles of religion, confessions of faith, creeds, &c. &c. &c. composed by men." "The New Testament has been as the law once was, *among the rubbish,*" proclaimed Smith. "Now we have found it, let us read it to the people from morning till

[50] Smith devoted a sermon of over 120 pages to the subject of how republican values should be applied to the church. See Elias Smith, *The Whole World Governed by a Jew; or the Government of the Second Adam, as King and Priest* (Exeter, N.H., 1805). On the Standing Order's conservative use of millennial themes, see Nathan O. Hatch, *The Sacred Cause of Liberty: Republican Thought and the Millennium in Revolutionary New England* (New Haven, 1977), 97-138. See also Richard M. Rollins, *The Long Journey of Noah Webster* (Philadelphia, 1980).

[51] James West Davidson, *The Logic of Millennial Thought: Eighteenth-Century New England* (New Haven, 1977), 122-41.

evening."[52] These were fighting words, no doubt, to the genteel clergy, men accustomed to covenants being the linchpin of society and to thinking of America as the new Israel. But even more radical than dismissing the Old Testament as a priestly rag used to hoodwink the people was the approach that Christians used to interpret Scripture. "I have endeavored to read the scriptures as though no one had read them before me," claimed Alexander Campbell, "and I am as much on my guard against reading them to-day, through the medium of my own views yesterday, or a week ago, as I am against being influenced by any foreign name, authority, or system whatever." Protestants had always argued for *sola scriptura*, but this kind of radical individualism set the Bible against the entire history of biblical interpretation. In this hermeneutic, no human authority, contemporary or historical, had the right to advise the individual in his spiritual quest. In order to ward off any systematic theology, these men insisted that religious discussion be limited to Bible language, as Smith put it, "to prove every particular from plain declarations recorded in the Bible."[53]

This fresh hermeneutic had considerable appeal because it spoke to three pressing issues. First, it proclaimed a new ground of certainty for a generation perplexed that it could no longer hear the voice of God above the din of sectarian confusion. If people would only abandon the husks of theological abstraction, the truth would be plain for all to see. Second, this approach to Scripture dared the common man to open the Bible and think for himself. All theological abstractions—such as the Trinity, foreordination, and original sin—were abandoned, and all that was necessary to establish a given point was to string together texts from the King James Bible. Any Christian using New Testament words could fend off the most brilliant theological argument by the simple retort that he was using God's word against human opinion. All the weight of church history could not begin to tip the

---

[52] *Herald of Gospel Liberty,* June 23, 1809, p. 87, Feb. 2, 1809, p. 47. The Christians repeatedly suggested that Americans accord the New Testament the same kind of exclusive authority that they did constitutions in civil affairs. See Smith, *World Governed by a Jew,* 114; and Campbell, *Declaration and Address of the Christian Association,* 16.

[53] *Christian Baptist,* April 3, 1826, p. 229; Smith, *Life,* 292.

scale against the Christian's simple declaration, say, that the New Testament did not contain the word *trinity*.

This approach had a third appeal—obvious success in befuddling the respectable clergy. Smith, O'Kelly, Stone, and Alexander Campbell were to a man brilliant theological debaters, but they refused to abide by the etiquette of the opposition. Their coarse language, earthy humor, biting sarcasm, and common sense reasoning appealed to the uneducated but left the professional clergy without a ready defense. In a pamphlet written in 1817 to combat Smith's influence in Massachusetts, the Congregationalist Thomas Andros recognized the new tactics:

> Ridicule, sneer, malignant sarcasm and reproach, are the armor in which he goes forth. On this ground, and not on sober argumentation, he knows the success of his cause depends. . . . If he knows the doctrine of original sin is not true, let him sit down and write a manly and candid answer to President Edward's great work on that subject. . . . Were he a dignified, candid, and intelligent controversialist, there would be enough to answer him, but who would wish to attack a windmill? Who can refute a sneer?

Andros also recognized that popularity rather than virtue was the clarion call of the movement: "They measure the progress of religion by the numbers, who flock to their standard; not by the prevalence of faith, and piety, justice and charity, and the public virtues in society in general."[54]

Other Congregationalists and Presbyterians, less sensitive to the new measures, continued to use the language of orthodoxy to lambaste the Christians as a new form of the threadbare heresies of Arius, Pelagius, and Socinius.[55] The Christians merely sidestepped these attacks by putting the disputed points before their followers and letting them choose

---

54 Andros, *Scriptures Liable to be Wrested to Men's Own Destruction*, 21, 6.

55 Porter, *Discourse in Two Parts*, 14; Rice, *Epistle to the Citizens of Kentucky*, 9-12.

between the language of Scripture and that of metaphysical subtlety. This democratic revolution in theology wrenched the queen of the sciences from the learned speculations of Harvard, Yale, and Princeton men and encouraged the blacksmith, cooper, and tiller of the soil not only to experience salvation but also to explain the process. Its genius was to allow common people to feel, for a fleeting moment at least, that they were beholden to no one and masters of their own fate.

How does one explain the theology of the people that came to be championed between 1790 and 1815? What kind of cultural context gave rise to similar movements in New England, the South, and the Midwest? Many historians have imagined that these radical pietists simply continued a tradition of dissent that had rippled through American culture since the 1740s. Others have viewed the Christians as prophets of the American frontier, men who developed notions in keeping with the self-sufficient characters that pushed into the hill country of New England and made their way across the Appalachians. This was religion following the frontier par excellence. Still other scholars have linked the Christian movement to the general revolt against Calvinism that followed the American Revolution. Rigid notions of depravity and predestination simply could not stir a generation that had witnessed at home and abroad the electrifying effects of liberty and natural rights. All of these—the ongoing tradition of evangelical dissent, the surge westward after the Revolution, and the disdain for Calvinistic explanations of the world—figure importantly in any explanation of the Christian movement. [56]

Yet these points of reference fail to locate the most intimate link between the Christians and American culture at the turn of the eighteenth century: a pervasive collapse of certainty within popular culture. From the debate over the

[56] William G. McLoughlin views the later wave of dissent as but an extension of the revivalism of the Great Awakening. McLoughlin, *New England Dissent,* II, 697-750. William Warren Sweet described the Christians as "a new denomination which arose directly out of the soil of the west." William Warren Sweet, *Religion in the Development of American Culture, 1765-1840* (New York, 1952), 221; and Winfred Ernest Garrison, *Religion Follows the Frontier: A History* of *the Disciples of Christ* (New York, 1931). Sweet also links the Christians to the broader revolt against Calvinism.

Constitution to the election of Jefferson, a new and explicitly democratic revolution united many who were suspicious of power and many who were powerless in a common effort to pull down the cultural hegemony of a gentlemanly few. In a complex cultural process that historians have just begun to unravel, people on a number of fronts began to speak, write, and organize against the authority of mediating elites, of social distinctions, and of any human tie that did not spring from volitional allegiance.[57]

This crisis of confidence in a hierarchical, ordered society led to demands for fundamental reform in politics, law, and religion. In each of these areas, radical Jeffersonians, seizing upon issues close to the hearts of the people, resurrected "the spirit of 1776" to protest the control of elites and the force of tradition. Rhetoric that had once unified people across the social spectrum now drove a powerful wedge between rich and poor, elite and commoner, privileged classes and the people. Federalists, members of the bar, and the professional clergy heard the wisdom of the ages ridiculed as mere connivances of the powerful to maintain the status quo.

The violence of politics from 1780 to 1800, more than anything else, gave sharp definition to egalitarian impulses in American society. From the Revolution onwards, republican equality became a rallying cry for people seeking to challenge all sorts of political authority. Incidents in South Carolina, Massachusetts, and New York illustrate how thoroughly the "virtue" of subjection and deference was giving way to an itching, smarting, writhing awareness of inferiority. In 1784, the South Carolina legislature threatened William Thompson, a tavern keeper, with banishment from the state for insulting the eminent John Rutledge. Thompson responded with a newspaper article that blasted the claims of "self-exalted" characters like Rutledge who had "conceived me his inferior." Thompson refused to "comprehend the *inferiority*" and

[57] For the importance of the idea of volitional allegiance in this period, see James H. Kettner, *The Development of American Citizenship, 1608-1870* (Chapel Hill, 1978), 173-209. See also Gordon S. Wood, *The Creation of the American Republic, 1776-1787* (Chapel Hill, 1969), 483-99; Alfred F. Young, *The Democratic Republicans of New York: The Origins, 1763-1797* (Chapel Hill, 1967); and Edmund S. Morgan, *The Challenge of the American Revolution* (New York, 1976), 211-18.

denied the right of a conspicuous few to speak for the people.[58] During the debate over the Constitution, Antifederalists turned repeatedly to such arguments. At the Massachusetts ratification convention, for example, the self-taught Worcester County farmer Amos Singletary denounced the Constitution as a plot to consolidate the influence of the great: "these lawyers and men of learning, and moneyed men . . . talk so finely, and gloss over matters so smoothly, to make us poor illiterate people swallow down the pill . . . . They expect to be the managers of this Constitution, and get all the power and all the money into their own hands. And then they will swallow up us little fellows, like the great Leviathan."[59]

A decade later the urban democratic leader William Keteltas was able to shake Federalist control of New York City by a shrewd media campaign depicting politics as a clash between rich and poor. Keteltas made into a cause celèbre the case of two Irish-born ferrymen whom Federalist magistrates punished summarily for reportedly insulting one of their number. Keteltas dramatized the issue in the popular press and eventually came to attack the New York assembly for not impeaching the responsible magistrates. This led to his own arrest by the Federalist legislature on a charge of breach of privilege. When Keteltas appeared before the assembly, a crowd of several thousand gathered in protest. His release from a brief prison sentence prompted a grand celebration in which the people pulled Keteltas through the streets in a carriage decked with American and French flags, a cap of liberty, and a picture of a man being whipped with the inscription, "What you rascal, insult your superiors?" By championing the cause of the ferrymen—what Keteltas called "the most flagrant abuse of [the people's] rights' since Independence" he effectively mobilized the common people of New York to challenge Federalist domination.[60]

Such repeated attacks on the capacity of a conspicuous

---

[58] Wood, *Creation of the American Republic*, 482-83.

[59] Jonathan Elliot, *The Debates, Resolutions, and Other Proceedings, in Convention on the Adoption of the Federal Constitution* (4 vols., Washington, D.C., 1827-1830), I, 112.

[60] Young, *Democratic Republicans of New York*, 468-95.

few to speak for the whole of society struck at the root of traditional conceptions of society.[61] Extending the logic of Antifederalists, radical Jeffersonians came to ridicule the assumption that society was an organic hierarchy of ranks and degrees; they argued, rather, that it was a heterogeneous mixture of many different classes, orders, interest groups, and occupations. In such a society the elites could no longer claim to be adequate spokesmen for people in general. In this climate, it took little creativity for some to begin to reexamine the social function of the clergy and to question the right of any order of men to claim authority to interpret God's Word. If opinions about politics and society were no longer the monopoly of the few, why could not anyone and everyone begin to think for themselves in matters of religion?

The 1790s also witnessed fundamental challenges to the legal profession and the common law. Richard E. Ellis has documented the strident attacks against the legal system that surfaced in the popular press and in serious political movements to reform the law in Kentucky, Pennsylvania, and Massachusetts.[62] Radical republicans such as Boston's Austin denounced the legal profession for needlessly confusing court cases in order to charge high fees, deliberately making the law inaccessible to laymen, bartering justice to those who could afford to pay, and monopolizing legislative and judicial posts.

Those who called for radical legal reform addressed three primary issues. First, they demanded a simplified and easily accessible legal process, "a system of laws of our own, dictated by the genuine principles of Republicanism, and made easy to be understood to every individual in the community."[63] Second, they attempted to replace the common law—authority by precedent—with fresh legal codes designed for the new republic. For many of these

---

[61] Wood, *Creation of the American Republic*, 483-99. One of the clearest calls that common people should resist the traditional distinction between gentlemen and commoners came from the pen of the uneducated Massachusetts farmer William Manning in 1798. Samuel Eliot Morrison, ed., "William Manning's *The Key of Libberty*," *William and Mary Quarterly*, XIII (April 1956), 202-54.

[62] Ellis, *Jeffersonian Crisis*.

[63] Benjamin Austin, Jr., "Observations on the Pernicious Practice of the Law" (1786), in *American Journal of Legal History*, XIII (July 1969), 258.

radicals, the common law conjured up images of complexity, mystery, intolerance, and bias in favor of the elite: "Shall we be directed by reason, equity, and a few simple and plain laws, promptly executed, or shall we be ruled by volumes of statutes and cases decided by the ignorance and intolerance of former times?"[64] Third, having jettisoned the "monkist priesthood" of lawyers and the "absurdity of the common law," those who sought root-and-branch reform exhibited great faith in the ability of ordinary citizens to ascertain and dispense justice before the law. "Any person of common abilities," said Austin, "can easily distinguish between right and wrong" and "more especially when the parties are admitted to give a plain story, without any puzzle from lawyers."[65]

In retrospect, this faith in democratic, personalized, and simplified law appears hopelessly naïve and utopian. Yet it reflects a moment of historical optimism, a time when many in politics, law, and religion, flushed with the promise of the American Revolution, found it reasonable to take literally the meaning of *novus ordo seclorum* and to declare a decisive expatriation from the past.[66]

That Smith came to jettison orthodox Calvinism through reading Austin's articles in the *Independent Chronicle* in 1799 and 1800 underscores the correlation between the Christian movement and reform efforts in politics and law.[67] In method, substance, and style, Smith championed the cause to which radical Jeffersonians were committed: an appeal to class as the fundamental problem of society, a refusal to recognize the cultural authority of elites, a disdain for the supposed lessons of history and tradition, a call for reform using the rhetoric of the Revolution, a commitment to turn the press into a sword of democracy, and an ardent faith in the future of the

---

64 "Decius," *Independent Chronicle*, Jan. 30, 1804, p. 1.

65 Ellis, *Jeffersonian Crisis*, 171, 177; Austin, "Observations on the Pernicious Practice of the Law," 264.

66 For the importance in Thomas Jefferson's thought of breaking the grip of custom and precedent, see Edmund S. Morgan, *The Meaning of Independence: John Adams, George Washington, Thomas Jefferson* (Charlottesville, 1976), 71-79; and Daniel J. Boorstin, *The Lost World of Thomas Jefferson* (Boston, 1948).

67 Smith, *Lovingkindness of God Displayed*, 32.

American republic. Smith's primary interest, of course, was the spread of evangelical religion; yet he could never divorce that message from the egalitarian principles that the frantic pace of the 1790s had made self-evident.

That other individuals came to advocate virtually identical reform is further evidence that questions were raging in popular culture that popular religion simply could not avoid. While other claims to truth also flourished in this atmosphere, the Christian movement stands out as an attempt to bring some harmony between denominational traditions and egalitarian values. In lashing out at the tyranny of the clergy, the foolishness of abstract theology, and the bondage of church discipline, the Christians fulfilled a mandate for reform that was widespread in popular culture. In exalting the idea that every man was his own interpreter, they brought a measure of certainty to people committed to the principle that all values, rights, and duties originate in the individual—the principle that Alexis de Tocqueville later called individualism.[68]

The legacy of the Christian movement is riddled with irony. Instead of taking America by storm, the Christian Connection under Smith and O'Kelly vanished into insignificance while the Disciples in the West grew into a major denomination only by practicing the kind of organization they had once hoped to stamp out. Instead of calming sectarian strife and restoring edenic harmony, the Christians engendered controversy at every step and had to put up with chronic factionalism within their own ranks.[69] Instead of offering a new foundation for certainty, the Christian approach to knowledge, which made no man the judge of another's conscience, had little holding power and

---

[68] Alexis de Tocqueville, *Democracy in America*, trans. Henry Reeve (2 vols., New York, 1959), I, 104-05.

[69] For an excellent example of the potential for factionalism within a local Christian church, see Don Harrison Doyle, *The Social Order of a Frontier Community: Jacksonville, Illinois, 1825-70* (Urbana, 1978), 157-60.

sent many early advocates scrambling for surer footing.[70] Instead of erecting a primitive church free from theological tradition and authoritarian control, the Christians came to advocate their own sectarian theology and to defer to the influence and persuasion of a dominant few. These ironies suggest that the real significance of the Christian movement is not to be found in its institutional development or in the direct influence of Smith, O'Kelly, Stone, and Alexander Campbell. What the movement does illustrate graphically is a moment of wrenching change in American culture that had great import for popular religion. Many followed the path even if they did not know its trailblazers.

The Christian movement illustrates, in the first place, the intensity of religious ferment at work in a period of chaos and originality unmatched, perhaps, since the religious turbulence of seventeenth-century England.[71] As in England a century and a half before, common folk in America at the dawn of the nineteenth century came to scorn tradition, relish novelty and experimentation, grope for fresh sources of authority, and champion an array of millennial schemes, each in its own way dethroning hierarchy and static religious forms.[72] The resulting popular culture pulsated with the claims of supremely heterodox religious groups, with people veering from one sect to another, with the unbridled wrangling of competitors in a "war of words."[73] Scholars have

---

[70] Smith himself left the Christian Connection in 1818 to join the Universalists, and two of his colleagues, Joshua V. Himes and Joseph Marsh, became early advocates of William Miller. David L. Rowe, "A New Perspective on the Burned-Over District: The Millerites in Upstate New York," *Church History*, XLVII (Dec. 1978), 408-20. Of five men who signed the "Last Will and Testament of Springfield Presbytery," two returned to the Presbyterians, two became Shakers, and only Stone retained his identity as a Christian. Alexander Campbell, similarly, saw his best preacher, Sidney Rigdon, defect to the Mormons. Mario S. De Pillis, "The Quest for Religious Authority and the Rise of Mormonism," *Dialogue: A Journal of Mormon Thought*, I (Spring 1966), 68-88.

[71] Christopher Hill, *The World Turned Upside Down: Radical Ideas during the English Revolution* (New York, 1972).

[72] J. F. C. Harrison, *The Second Coming: Popular Millenarianism, 1780-1850* (New Brunswick, 1979), 163-206.

[73] The phrase is that of Joseph Smith, who reacted strongly to the sectarian competition he knew as a young man. Joseph Smith, *The Pearl of Great Price* (Salt Lake City, 1891), 56-70. In this period evangelicals were preoccupied with a sense of the transforming power of the printed word. See Joan Jacobs Brumberg, *Mission For Life: The Story of the Family of Adoniram Judson* (New York, 1980), 44-78.

only begun to assess the fragmentation that beset American religion in the period generally referred to as the Second Great Awakening, which they have too often viewed as a conservative response to rapid social change. The Christian movement serves as a helpful corrective and invites fresh appraisals of the popular culture that nourished people like William Miller, John Humphrey Noyes, and Joseph Smith. Theirs was a religious environment that brought into question traditional authorities and exalted the right of the people to think for themselves. The result, quite simply, was a bewildering world of clashing opinion—to the sympathetic Smith, an "age of inquiry," to the distraught David Rice, a "hot bed of every extravagance of opinion and practice." Another erstwhile pilgrim, the Presbyterian-turned-Christian-turned-Shaker Richard McNemar, took up verse to capture the spirit of his times:

> Ten thousand Reformers like so many moles
> Have plowed all the Bible and cut it [in] holes
> And each has his church at the end of his trace
> Built up as he thinks of the subjects of grace.[74]

The Christians also illustrate the exaltation of public opinion as a primary religious authority. They called for common folk to read the New Testament as if mortal man had never seen it before. People were expected to discover the self-evident message of the Bible without any mediation from creeds, theologians, or clergymen not of their own choosing. This explicit faith that biblical authority could emerge from below, from the will of the people, was the most enduring legacy of the Christian movement. By the 1840s one analyst of American Protestantism concluded, after surveying fifty-three American sects, that the principle "No creed but the Bible" was the distinctive feature of American religion. John W. Nevin surmised that this emphasis grew out of a

[74] Elias Smith, *The Age of Enquiry* (Exeter, N.H., 1807); David Rice, "A Second Epistle to the Citizens of Kentucky, Professing the Christian Religion," in *An Outline of the History of the Church in the State of Kentucky,* ed. Robert Bishop (Lexington, Ky., 1824), 354; Richard McNemar, "The Mole's Little Pathways" as quoted in De Pillis, "Quest for Religious Authority," 75.

popular demand for "private judgment" and was "tacitly if not openly conditioned always by the assumption that every man is authorized and bound to get at this authority in a direct way for himself, through the medium simply of his own single mind."[75] Many felt the exhilarating hope that democracy had opened an immediate access to biblical truth for all persons of good will. What was difficult for Americans to realize was that a commitment to private judgment could drive people apart even as it raised beyond measure their hopes for unity.

The Christian movement also demonstrates the process by which popular culture became christianized in the early republic. One reason that evangelical churches and sects grew so rapidly during these years was that they proclaimed value systems that endowed common people with dignity and responsibility. People gladly accepted a theology that addressed them without condescension, balked at vested interests, and reinforced ideas of volitional allegiance and self-reliance. While such egalitarian strains were deeply rooted in the Great Awakening and subsequent revivals, historians have failed to appreciate the ways in which the founding of the American republic wrought, in Devereux Jarratt's words, "a vast alteration" in American religion. A staunch evangelical minister in Virginia prior to the Revolution, Jarratt by the 1790s had come to fear the volatile mix of things evangelical and egalitarian. Bemoaning the "levelling" spirit in "our high republican times," Jarratt recoiled from a religion "under the supreme controul of tinkers and taylors, weavers, shoemakers, and country mechanics of all kinds."[76] The theology that emerged between 1790 and 1815 to empower just these kinds of people certainly helps to clarify a process by which an America that had been largely Presbyterian, Congregational, Anglican, and Calvinist Baptist became a cauldron of Methodists, Disciples, Freewill, Free-Communion, and Primitive Baptists, Universalists, Mormons, and Millerites—to name a

[75] John Williamson Nevin, "Antichrist and the Sect," in *The Mercersburg Theology,* ed. James Hastings Nichols (New York, 1966), 93-119, 98-99.

[76] Devereux Jarratt, *The Life of the Reverend Devereux Jarratt* (Baltimore, 1806), 14-15, 181.

few. This new religious culture, which sanctioned the right of the individual to go his own way, would have been unthinkable apart from the crisis of authority in popular culture that accompanied the birth of the American republic.

# The Sectional Origins of Churches of Christ

**David Edwin Harrell, Jr.**

One of the new churches spawned by the religious ferment in early nineteenth-century America was the Disciples of Christ. Biblical literalists with an activistic faith, the early Disciples preached a "restoration of the ancient gospel"; their central plea was "to speak where the Bible speaks and be silent where the Bible is silent." By the early 1830s the Disciples of Christ had emerged as an independent denomination and, under the capable and energetic leadership of Alexander Campbell, made impressive gains during the decades between 1830 and 1860. On the eve of the Civil War the church had a membership of well over 200,000. The rapid growth of the movement continued unabated after the war. By 1880 the number of Disciples exceeded half a million, and by the first decade of the twentieth century the church had well over a million members.[1]

The nineteenth-century growth of the Disciples was accompanied by the development of serious internal tensions. Although nominally the movement remained united until the religious census of 1906 that listed separately the Disciples of Christ and the Churches of Christ, this official report was little more than a belated acknowledgment of an accomplished fact. For over half a century before 1906 the group had been divided into factions debating such doctrinal issues as the use of instrumental music in worship services, missionary societies, and the pastor system. No official pronouncement of schism had been made because there was no authoritative organization to issue one; but most church-

[1] The two standard studies of the church are Winfred E. Garrison and Alfred T. DeGroot, *The Disciples of Christ* (St. Louis, 1948) and Earl Irvin West, *The Search for the Ancient Order* (2 vols., Nashville, 1957). See also, for a sociological interpretation of the movement, Oliver Read Whitley, *Trumpet Call of Reformation* (St. Louis, 1959).

related institutions, editors of church periodicals, preachers, and local churches had aligned themselves with one faction or the other by the beginning of the twentieth century.

Division within the Disciples had roots deep in the nineteenth century. From the beginning of its organization in the 1830s the group had contained both men of moderate, unexcitable character and a more colorful array of unsophisticated exhorters. The dual plea of the early leaders of the church for the "restoration of the ancient order of things" and "Christian unity" lent itself to conflicting emphases. While most of the early reformers insisted that both ends must be accomplished before the millennium could begin, it became increasingly apparent that the extremely sectarian element in the group considered the legalistic restoration principle more important, while the more denominationally-oriented liberals believed that the principle of Christian unity was primary. As the initial fervor of the pioneer venture began to wane, as a sense of denominational responsibility began to grow among the more influential church leaders, and as a loose denominational organization began to emerge, it was inevitable that the discordant elements within the group should go their separate ways. The specific doctrinal issues that arose were only incidental. If Disciples had not disagreed over instrumental music and missionary societies, they would have divided over something else, as from the beginning the movement had attracted people of antipodal sociological and psychological backgrounds.

The two major groups that emerged are best identified by their institutional loyalties. The liberals in the church were known as "society men" or "*Standard* men" to identify them as backers of the American Christian Missionary Society and the leading liberal journal of the 1870s, the *Christian Standard*. On the other hand, the conservatives were called "antis" or "*Advocate* men," which marked them as opponents of the society and supporters of the most powerful of the Southern conservative periodicals, the *Gospel Advocate*. More and more the name Churches of Christ came to be quasi-official among the Southern conservatives and the name Christian Church among the more liberal Northern members of the movement. While the name Disciples of Christ was more widely used in the North, it continued to be acceptable in both sections and remains the most useful term to describe the entire movement.[2]

The conservative wing of the divided movement, the Churches of Christ, has grown very rapidly in the half century since 1906. By 1961, according to the estimate in the most recent *Yearbook of American Churches*, the Churches of Christ had a membership of around 2,250,000.[3] Together with the more liberal segment of the movement, the Christian Church, it forms the largest and most significant religious movement native to America.

One of the most distinctive characteristics of the Churches of Christ from their beginning has been the marked sectional distribution of the membership.[4] According to the 1906 religious census, 101,734 of the churches' 159,658 members lived in the eleven former states of the Confederacy. Another 30,206 lived in the four border states of Kentucky, West Virginia, Missouri, and Oklahoma. The only state north of the Ohio River to have a membership of over 5,000 was Indiana.[5]

---

[2] The terminology in the Disciples movement is confusing. Actually, in both North and South all of the three names–*Disciples of Christ*, *Christian Church*, and *Churches of Christ*–are still used by both conservatives and liberals. In this study, the name *Churches of Christ* is used exclusively to denote the anti-instrumental-music conservatives. The term *Christian Church* is used to describe the Northern liberals. The name *Disciples of Christ* is most useful to describe the entire nebulous movement, although occasionally it appears as the official title of the liberal church.

[3] Benson Y. Landis (ed.), *Yearbook of American Churches* (New York, 1964), 255.

[4] Although it has been nearly three decades since a census of the group has been taken, a recent expert stated a self-evident fact when he described the church as a "predominantly Southern group." Wilbur Zelinsky, "An Approach to the Religious Geography of the United States: Patterns of Church Membership in 1942," Association of American Geographers, *Annals*, I.I (June 1961), 143. This judgment probably is becoming increasingly less true. The mobility of Southern population in recent years, along with the evangelistic efforts of the church, has created a more diverse pattern of membership. See Zelinsky's entire article for a sophisticated approach to religious geography. He ably discusses the reliability of various religious censuses. For the Disciples movement, the only available statistics are those reported in the four government censuses between 1906 and 1936. Although these studies are far from flawless, for the purposes of this study they are adequate.

[5] U.S. Bureau of the Census, . . . *Religious Bodies: 1906* . . . (2 vols., Washington, 1910), II, 240, 243. The Churches of Christ listed a membership of 10,259 in Indiana while the liberal Disciples of Christ reported 108,188. Even here, the more conservative wing of the movement controlled a relatively small part of the state. See below, notes 35 and 37, for a fuller discussion of Indiana and other states which fail to fit neatly into the sectional pattern.

These statistics are even more striking when compared with the membership distribution of the more liberal wing of the movement, that listed in the 1906 census as the Disciples of Christ. Only 138,703 of the total Disciples' membership of nearly a million lived in the eleven Southern states. Excluding Virginia and North Carolina, where the liberal Disciples won virtually all of the churches, the group had a total membership of only 99,233 in the remaining nine states.[6] In sum, while the Churches of Christ had little appeal to the members of the Campbell reform movement outside of the South, they were highly successful in capturing their share of the church within that section.[7]

The sectional bifurcation of the Disciples of Christ–using the name to refer to the whole movement–is one of the most vivid American examples of the bending of the Christian ethos to fit the presuppositions of the community. All of the complex antagonisms in nineteenth-century American society–North and South, East and West, urban and rural, affluent and dispossessed–left their marks on the theology and institutional development of the group. Schism was a result of differences far more complex than doctrinal disagreement–far more than the simple statement that "The 'Christian Churches' . . . took their instruments and their missionary society and walked a new course."[8] While it remains useful to define the schism within the movement doctrinally, the more fundamental question is, why did some

---

[6] See below, note 37, for a discussion of the course of the church in Virginia and North Carolina. According to the 1906 census, the Churches of Christ had a membership of only 415 in the two states.

[7] By the time the last official religious census was published in 1936, the sectional pattern in the divided movement had deepened. Of the 309,551 members listed by the Churches of Christ in 1936 over 192,000 lived in the eleven former Confederate states and another 65,000 lived in Kentucky, West Virginia, Missouri, and Oklahoma. Excluding Virginia and North Carolina, the Churches of Christ outnumbered the Disciples of Christ in the South by over 30,000. In terms of relative strength, the Churches of Christ gained on the Christian Church in nearly every Southern state during the thirty years between 1906 and 1936. U.S. Bureau of Census, . . . *Religious Bodies: 1936* . . . (3 vols., Washington, 1941), II, pt. 2, 464-66, 535-37.

[8] West, *Search for the Ancient Order*, II, 448. To state the truism that some people in the movement believed it was unscriptural to use instrumental music in worship services and to support missionary societies contributes little to an understanding of the origin of the Churches of Christ.

Disciples remain conservative while others were relaxing their doctrinal standards? Or even more pertinent: Why did such a large number of Southern Disciples oppose "innovations" while most Northern Disciples believed the scriptures authorized them? The obvious fact that the Churches of Christ are sectional (and, for that matter, so is the Northern-oriented Disciples church) leads to the obvious question: What are the sectional origins of the group?

The most likely place to look for the sectional origins of a church in the nineteenth century is in the wake of the bitter struggle centering around slavery and culminating in the Civil War. Historians of the Disciples have seriously underestimated the impact of these sectional pressures on the movement.[9] It is true, of course, that there were moderates in the church, as there were moderates in the nation. Foremost among them was the revered Alexander Campbell who worked feverishly to keep the social issue of slavery from destroying the religious movement he had initiated. Campbell and many other moderate Disciples leaders held to their views even during the war years, but after 1845, they had become more and more on the defensive against attacks from extremists in both sections.[10] One beleaguered moderate editor wrote in 1856, "We have been scolded, bemeaned,

---

[9] Robert Richardson, one of the earliest historians of the church, wrote in 1868, "Mr. Campbell's conservative course in regard to this disturbing question [slavery] . . . preserved the reforming churches from division." Robert Richardson, *Memoirs of Alexander Campbell* (2 vols., Philadelphia, 1868-1870), II, 534. Over sixty years later, a modern church historian wrote in a similar vein on the effect of Alexander Campbell's moderate stand on the slavery issue, "It cost him much criticism from both sides, but it established general lines of an attitude which not only saved the Disciples from a division in 1845, but enabled them to go through the Civil War still undivided." Winfred E. Garrison, *Religion Follows the Frontier* (New York, 1931), 179-80. See, for similar interpretations, Robert E. Barnes, An Analytical Study of the Northwestern Christian Magazine (unpublished B. D. thesis, School of Religion, Butler University, 1951), 126-30; Eileen Gordon Vandegrift, The Christian Missionary Society: A Study in the Influence of Slavery on the Disciples of Christ (unpublished M. A. thesis, Butler University, 1945), 81; and Robert O. Fife, Alexander Campbell and the Christian Church in the Slavery Controversy (unpublished Ph.D. thesis, University of Indiana, 1960), 255-73. See, for the opposite point of view and a general discussion of the Disciples and the slavery controversy, David Edwin Harrell, Jr., A Social History of the Disciples of Christ to 1866 (unpublished Ph.D. thesis, Vanderbilt University, 1962), 233-344.

[10] See Campbell's series of articles entitled, "Our Position to American Slavery," *Millennial Harbinger*, s. 3, II (January-August 1854). The best study of Campbell's social thought is Harold L. Lunger's *The Political Ethics of Alexander Campbell* (St. Louis, 1954).

threatened, and called a 'coward,' a 'dumb dog,' and a 'popularity seeker,' not because of what we *have* said, but because of what we have *not* said–because of our silence."[11]

Some of the earliest Disciples preachers were ardent antislavery advocates. In 1834, Nathaniel Field, an abolitionist preacher from Jeffersonville, Indiana, wrote that he had "resolved not to break the loaf with slaveholders or in any way to countenance them as Christians."[12] By the late 1850s many Disciples congregations in the North supported an abolitionist platform, and in 1857 John Boggs, who edited a militantly abolitionist Disciples monthly in Cincinnati, wrote, "Every congregation built on the Bible . . . would . . . prohibit the reception as members those who practice . . . slavery."[13]

A series of crises in the 1850s widened the breach between the radical antislavery element and the rest of the church. Abolitionist desire for a safe educational institution led to the establishment of North Western Christian University in Indianapolis in 1850. Four years later, frustrated by the suppression of controversial material by the moderate editors of the church, an antislavery religious periodical, the *North Western Christian Magazine*, was established in Cincinnati. From these institutional centers Disciples radicals inveighed against the sinfulness of the federal government and the silence of the moderates in the church and reserved special damnation for the course of the American Christian Missionary Society. The Society, which was the only national organization in the church and the outstanding symbol of church unity, was repeatedly condemned as "the pliant tool of the slave-holding aristocracy" because its leaders solicited funds among Southern churches and because of the

[11] Benjamin Franklin, "Where is the Safe Ground," *American Christian Review,* I (February 1856), 35.

[12] "Letter from Nat. Field, Jeffersonville," *Evangelist,* III (October 1834), 234.

[13] "Querist's Department," *North Western Christian Magazine,* IV (September 1857), 90. Such expressions were not uncommon. See, for example, A[lexander] C[ampbell], "An Excursion in Ohio," *Millennial Harbinger*, s. 4, VI (November 1857), 652; B. F. Perky, "News," *Gospel Proclamation*, II (May 1849), 549; John Rogers to Isaac Errett, November 6, 1851, in Disciples Manuscript Collection (Christian Theological Seminary Library, Indianapolis).

employment of a former slaveholder as a missionary to Jerusalem.[14]

A complete rupture between the radical abolitionists in the church and the American Christian Missionary Society came in 1859 when the society refused to support an outspoken antislavery preacher as a missionary in Kansas. Disciples extremists in the North were infuriated and in the following year organized a society of their own with an antislavery constitution. The new organization, named the Christian Missionary Society, was relatively weak but it was far from insignificant. The bolting abolitionists had able leadership, a periodical outlet, at least one educational institution supporting their cause, and the sympathy of many of the churches of the North.[15]

The Civil War by no means ended division within the church. Although it did bring the radical antislavery bolters back into the mainstream of the Northern church (or, more correctly, brought the Northern church to them), it generated new tensions that would not be eased so quickly.[16] While some churchmen in both sections remained aloof from the struggle, for the most part, Disciples North and Disciples

---

[14] James S. Lamar, *Memoirs of Isaac Errett* (2 vols., Cincinnati, 1893), I, 217.

[15] Eileen Vandegrift's thesis on the Christian Missionary Society is a very able study. Of course, it is impossible to say whether or not the abolitionist schism would have been permanent, but there is every reason to believe that it would have been. It would be possible to exaggerate the size of the bolting group, but not the reality of the rupture.

[16] The sectional impact of the Civil War on the church has been ignored almost completely by the historians of the movement. Winfred Garrison writes, "Its [Civil War's] ultimate effect was less divisive than might have been expected; in fact, not divisive at all." *Religion Follows the Frontier*, 221. Another recent scholar writes, "The churches . . . weathered the issues created by the war without any serious disruption." West, *Search for the Ancient Order*, I, 350. The nineteenth-century historian, William T. Moore, insisted that nothing "like a division" was "ever seriously contemplated by brethren on either side of the conflict." "Reformation of the Nineteenth Century, the Turbulent Period," *Christian Evangelist,* XXXVI (June 1, 1899), 680. This misjudgment has been passed down from one generation of Disciples of Christ historians to another. It has been based partly on a companion misjudgment on the prevalence of pacifism in the church. One historian reports that the church's leaders opposed the war "almost to a man." Glen W. Mell, a Study of the Opinions of Some Leading Disciples Concerning Pacifism (unpublished B. D. thesis, School of Religion, Butler University, 1936), 53-54. The more general literature on American religion reflects this distortion. John R. Bodo, in his *The Protestant Clergy and Public Issues, 1812-1848* (Princeton, 1954), 227, writes: "The Disciples of Christ . . . began as a pacifist sect. All of their leaders, with the exception of Walter Scott, were avowed pacifists." This interpretation of the movement is simply not true. Some of the leading preachers in the group were pacifists, but they by no means represented the majority of the church.

South preached and prayed as their sons fought and died. Within the organizational structure of the church the war deepened the already present sectional antagonisms into a pattern that could still be discerned clearly in the 1906 schism. The crucial event in this realignment of forces came in the convention of the American Christian Missionary Society in Cincinnati in 1863.

The 1863 convention met at a time when tensions within the church were strong. The moderates, led by the aging Alexander Campbell and a powerful Cincinnati editor, Benjamin Franklin, had succeeded in squashing an effort to pass resolutions of loyalty to the Union in the 1861 convention.[17] But the moderates never represented a majority of the opinion at that convention; prowar preachers had acquiesced, but their silence was sullen and begrudging. By the time of the 1863 convention, the compromising temper of the loyalists in the North had changed. They were determined to push through loyalty resolutions.[18] Northern preachers were particularly goaded by accusations of disloyalty leveled at the church and the missionary society by the secular press.[19] Even more pressing in the minds of some was the refusal of the abolitionist Christian Missionary Society to abandon its organizational schism unless such resolutions were passed.

The 1863 convention began with a rousing prowar speech by the corresponding secretary of the society and reached a climax with the passage by an overwhelming vote of resolutions repudiating the "reports [that] have gone abroad that we, as a religious body, and particularly as a Missionary Society, are to a certain degree disloyal to the Government of the United States." The society further "unqualifiedly declared" its "allegiance to said Government" and tendered its "sympathies to our brave and noble soldiers, who are

---

[17] Loyalty resolutions were "unofficially" passed at the 1861 convention. See American Christian Missionary Society, *Report of Proceedings of the Thirteenth Anniversary Meeting* . . . (Cincinnati, 1861), 19-20.

[18] Unionists insisted from the beginning that they represented the large majority of the church. "A Reply to 'Vindication of Ourselves and the Pioneer,'" *Christian Pioneer*, I (December 1861), 322-31; Elijah Goodwin, "A. C. Missionary Society," *Weekly Christian Record*, I (November 4, 1862), 2.

[19] "A Reply to 'Vindication of Ourselves and the Pioneer,'" 322-34.

defending us from the attempts of armed traitors to overthrow the Government."[20] The results of the loyalist triumph in the 1863 convention were predictable. The radicals in the North were pleased, and the renegade Christian Missionary Society was dissolved. By and large the church in the North was reunited.

On the other hand, it was immediately obvious that the sectional pronouncement would cause serious resentment in the border areas and in the South. Southern church leaders had no opportunity to express themselves publicly on the war resolution until 1866, but a number of influential preachers from the border areas immediately attacked the American Christian Missionary Society. John W. McGarvey, influential preacher from Lexington, Kentucky, wrote, "I have judged the American Christian Missionary Society, and have decided for myself, that it should now cease to exist."[21] His articles ripped open the festering sores of sectional bitterness. Opposition to the society spread through Kentucky. Aylette Rains, an eastern Kentucky preacher, tersely scribbled in his diary: "Bro. McGarvey has taken the position that the A. C. Missionary Society is dead!"[22]

In short, by the close of the Civil War the Disciples of Christ movement was deeply involved in the nation's sectional strife. The only question in 1865 was whether or not the nebulous unity of the movement could be restored—in spite of the seething sectional bitterness in the church. Was a rapprochement possible?

Hope for a cordial reunion was dampened by the appearance early in 1866 of two sectionally-oriented weekly church periodicals. By 1863 most Northern church leaders, joined by border state loyalists, had become openly critical of the neutral *American Christian Review*, and a number of them had begun to formulate plans for the establishment of a

---

20 American Christian Missionary Society, *Report of Proceedings of the Fifteenth Anniversary Meeting* . . . (Cincinnati, 1863), 24.

21 "Missionary Societies," *American Christian Quarterly Review*, II ([November?], 1863), 342.

22 Diary, December 27, 1863, in Aylette Rains Papers (College of the Bible Library, Lexington).

Unionist paper.[23] These plans led to the founding in April 1866 of the *Christian Standard,* edited by Isaac Errett, one of the most respected churchmen of the North. It had the financial backing of such outstanding Northern laymen as Representative James A. Garfield and the wealthy Thomas W. Phillips of New Castle, Pennsylvania.

Unquestionably the *Standard* was founded out of sectional interest. Shortly after the close of the war, the editor of the paper told the powerful Southern preacher, David Lipscomb, that the journal was begun so that the "loyal brethren" would have somewhere to "express themselves . . . on the duty of Christians to support the government in its war upon the rebellion, its duty to punish traitors, and to express themselves on the infamy of slavery."[24]

More significant evidence of the growing sectional division is found in the *Gospel Advocate*, a Nashville weekly that resumed publication in January 1866 after an interruption of four years. David Lipscomb and Tolbert Fanning, the editors of the paper, denounced the activities of the church in the North during the war: "Those brethren who believe that political resolutions are the Gospel can do so; and those who desire to contribute to such an object can do so; *we cannot do it.*"[25] It became increasingly obvious that the editors of the *Advocate* were making a thinly veiled appeal for backing to the supporters of the lost cause. Isaac Errett charged that the *Gospel Advocate* "commenced its new issue with an appeal to

---

23 D. Pat Henderson to Isaac Errett, November 21, 1861; William Baxter to Errett, December 16, 1863; John Rogers to Errett, August 10, 1863; and R. Milligan to Errett, October 29, 1863, all in Disciples Manuscript Collection.

24 "The Truth of History," *Gospel Advocate,* XXXIV (July 14, 1892), 436. Lipscomb is hardly an unbiased authority on the founding of the *Christian Standard,* but there is little reason to doubt that this conversation is accurately reported. John W. McGarvey's description of the motivations behind the establishment of the journal may be fairer: "After the death of Mr. Campbell and the subsequent suspension of the Harbinger, there soon arose a strong feeling among the leading brethren in the northern States, in favor of a weekly paper of higher literary merit than the *American Christian Review* then conducted by Benjamin Franklin and exerting a powerful influence throughout the brotherhood, and one which would be more 'loyal' as the phrase went, to the Federal Government then engaged in the struggle of the civil war." J. W. McGarvey, *Autobiography* (Lexington, 1960), 73.

25 "A Reply to the Call of W. C. Rogers, Corresponding Secretary of the A. C. M. Society for All to Disseminate the Gospel," *Gospel Advocate*, VIII (March 27, 1866), 109.

men of southern blood, and proposed cooperation among them only. It has constantly denounced the brethren of the North who shared in the military defense of the government."[26] For the next several decades the editors of the *Advocate* rarely missed an opportunity to remind the Disciples of the South that the editor of the *Standard* and other Northern church leaders had been "strong Union men" during the war.[27]

The most revealing facet of the postwar sectional agitation within the church was the persistent practice of both Northern and Southern church leaders of linking their sectional prejudices with their theological convictions. The doctrinal positions that eventually became the outward distinguishing marks of the Christian Church and the Churches of Christ were clearly and consciously tied to the sectional pressures in the nation. Especially in the South it was not unusual for orthodoxy to include both theological conservatism and Southern sectional values.

The strongly loyalist action of the American Christian Missionary Society during the war virtually assured that it would be the center of a sectionally-oriented theological controversy when the struggle ended.[28] Although purely biblical arguments soon abounded on both sides of the missionary society controversy, the sectional coloration remained strong. Lanceford B. Wilkes, one of the leading Kentucky conservatives, wrote in 1870: "I am opposed to the Cincinnati society. . . . The society's political raid is regretted, I have reason to think, by its best friends."[29] A large portion of the church in Texas refused to support the formation of a state missionary society in 1892 because it was "as specifically an

---

[26] "The Gospel Advocate," *Christian Standard*, II (February 16, 1867), 52.

[27] See, for a discussion of this facet of the struggle, David Edwin Harrell, Jr., "Disciples of Christ Pacifism in Nineteenth Century Tennessee," *Tennessee Historical Quarterly*, XXI (September 1962), 263-74.

[28] It should be said that there was some theological opposition to the missionary society prior to the Civil War, and it would have unquestionably been a source of friction had it not become involved in the sectional struggle. But the course that the society controversy did follow was without a doubt influenced by the society's wartime activities.

[29] "L. B. Wilkes Sets Himself Right on Missionary Societies," *American Christian Review*, X (September 3, 1867), 285.

ecclesiasticism as the Baptist association or the Methodist conference" and because those who promoted the project were "following northern ideas and northern men."[30]

Northern editors repeatedly charged church leaders of the South with trying to propagate theological conservatism by fanning sectional prejudice. One preacher reported that a minister from "Yankeedom" could not even get a hearing in Texas, and accusations that "a few" Southern editors were trying to "run a Mason and Dixon line through the Bible and Church of Christ" were frequent by the 1890s.[31] The complaints of Northern churchmen were not without justification. A fiery Southern preacher argued that "neither Tennessee nor Texas would have had any progressive foolishness" if it had not been for the invasion of "carpetbag pastors" from the North.[32] Thomas R. Burnett, vitriolic Texas "anti," summed up the conservative sectional gospel in 1892: "We know the doctrine advocated by them [writers in the *Christian Standard*] comes from the *North*. It is neither scriptural nor *Southern*, and is not suited to Southern people. But it is the determination of the *Standard* and its *Northern* allies . . . to force the new things upon the churches of this section."[33] Burnett's reasoning was effective in the South of the 1890s.

The heritage of bitterness was not the only force that shaped much of the South into a cultural and religious unit in post-Civil War society. The South also displayed an economic homogeneity well into the twentieth century; and, in spite of rumblings of a New South, the hero image in Southern society remained the simple and austere yeoman farmer. In

---

30 "Our Budget," *Christian Evangelist*, XXIX (July 28, 1892), 472.

31 "No North or South in Christ," *Missionary Weekly*, XII (February 26, 1891), 4; "From the Papers," *Gospel Advocate*, XXXIII (March 25, 1891), 177.

32 T. R. Burnett, "Burnett's Budget," *Gospel Advocate*, XXXVIII (November 26, 1896), 755.

33 "Our Budget," *Christian Evangelist*, XXIX (July 21, 1892), 456. In the same article, the editor of the *Christian Evangelist* wrote a discerning analysis of the sectional background of the doctrinal conflict in the church: "And after all, with the great majority of the members of the church in the South, for it is in the South that the opposition to cooperative mission work is strongest, the chief reason for suspecting and opposing missionary work has been all along and now is that its headquarters and chief supporters have been in the north and west." *Ibid.*, 472.

the meanwhile, in much of the North, the "Second American Revolution" wrought dramatic changes, not only in the industrialization of the section but also in the minds of the people. The businessman became the new idol, and financial success was equated with diligence, ability, and godliness. Diverging economic patterns combined with postwar bitterness to widen the sectional rift.

The relation of characteristic economic patterns, North and South, to the origins of the Churches of Christ is easily demonstrated. The 1936 religious census, recording urban and rural membership, points up one significant feature. In the Northern-dominated Disciples of Christ nearly 750,000 of the group's 1,196,315 members were classified as urban. On the other hand, over 175,000 of the Churches of Christ's 309,551 members were affiliated with rural churches.[34] In most of the Southern states the membership of the Disciples of Christ was overwhelmingly urban; in the Churches of Christ, rural membership outnumbered urban in nine of the eleven former states of the Confederacy.[35]

Even more impressive are the census estimates of the value of church edifices in each state. For the Churches of Christ the total value of church edifices divided by the total number of congregations amounted to less than $3,000; the comparable figure for the Disciples of Christ was nearly $16,000.[36] This superiority of the Disciples, as measured by the average value of church property per congregation, was substantial in every state. For example, in Georgia the average for the Disciples of Christ was around $12,000 and for the Churches of Christ $4,500; in Kentucky the Disciples

[34] *Religious Bodies: 1936*, II, pt. 2, 464, 535. A recent estimate that "about 80% of the Churches of Christ are in rural areas" is certainly incorrect. *Encyclopedia Britannica* (1962), V, 675. The Churches of Christ have been a part of the baggage of thousands of Southerners who made the exodus into urban centers all over the country since World War II.

[35] The four states in the South where Disciples rural membership outnumbered urban membership were Virginia, North Carolina, South Carolina, and Georgia. Virginia and North Carolina are discussed below, note 37. In South Carolina the combined membership of both Disciples and Churches of Christ was less than 3,000. Urban membership was greater for both churches in Georgia. In Indiana, the strongest Churches of Christ state outside the South, the figures showed 9,058 rural members and 3,794 urban. In the same state the large Disciples of Christ membership was well over fifty percent urban.

[36] This figure has no particular meaning in itself, but it serves as a useful yardstick.

led $13,500 to $2,500; in Tennessee, $14,000 to $3,000; in Texas, $20,000 to $3,500; and in Indiana, $13,000 to $2,300.[37] The meaning of these figures is obvious. The conservative Churches of Christ preachers of the South were identified not only with a sectional audience but also with an economic class.

The economic pattern so obvious in the 1936 religious census is discernible also in the writings of nineteenth-century Disciples leaders. The churches in the North, especially in the urban centers, became markedly more genteel in the decades following the Civil War. The successful businessman became the financial, and often the spiritual, dictator of middle-class congregations. The church in the South continued to be dominated by an agricultural outlook, and its theology smacked strongly of anti-aristocratic prejudices. All of the doctrinal issues involved in the division of the movement–organized mission work, instrumental music, the pastor system–required congregations to make a decision that concerned not only their faith but also their finances.

By the 1870s there is good evidence of the growing class consciousness in the church. In the 1871 convention of the American Christian Missionary Society, Benjamin U. Watkins, an acrimonious old conservative, shocked the assembly with a speech in which he suggested that most of the young preachers in the church were looking for "stylish places to preach in, rich congregations to minister to, and

[37] It is precisely at this point that Virginia and North Carolina, that simply do not fit into a North-South or a rural-urban interpretation of the Disciples schism, fall into place. The average value of church property per congregation in Virginia was over $10,000, and in North Carolina it was over $8,000. The churches of these states belong in the same category with those of such states as Kentucky, Missouri, Indiana, and Illinois, where the movement contained large, prosperous rural memberships. This element refused to follow the radical leadership of the sectarian conservatives of the deep South, although it shared many of the prejudices of the radicals. But while these churches remained in the main body of the Disciples, they never really accepted the leadership of the urban liberals. Although no historian has studied the problem, it seems obvious that this is the sociological setting for the twentieth century Independent-Co-operative schism in the Disciples of Christ. One final qualification needs to be made in accounting for the local success of the various pleas within the restoration movement. It would be foolish to discount completely the personal influence of many magnetic preachers and editors. But, when all is said and done, these men were influenced by their sociological environment, and their leadership was effective because they fit the pattern demanded by their society.

positions . . . among those who [have] large and well-filled pockets." He insisted the poor ought to be the "special object" of Christianity. Lewis L. Pinkerton, a Kentucky liberal, led a counterattack. Pinkerton asserted that "the most beautiful souls it had been his privilege to know–those who best illustrated meekness and gentleness . . . [were] not among the poor but the rich." He doubted "if Christianity could take root and flourish in the wretched, filthy, vermin-besieged houses of the poor of Cincinnati, or elsewhere."[38]

More often than not the class conflict within the church pitted agricultural poverty against urban middle-class-affluence. "The modern rendering of the great commission," wrote a disgruntled rural layman in 1894, "appears to be, Go into the large cities and preach the Gospel, or go where the people will pay a good salary and entertain the preacher in good style." He complained that the "city preachers" were "continually begging in the country to build houses of worship in the cities."[39]

There was ample evidence to demonstrate the domination of the Northern church by urban congregations, business leaders, and middle-class religious norms. The most sought-after preacher was the man whose "motto is vim, vigor and victory."[40] A leading Northern preacher suggested the "greatest need" in the church was the use of "*strictly business principles* in our religious enterprises."[41] In 1894 the Board of Church Extension began publication of a quarterly magazine entitled *Business in Christianity*, that, according to its promoters, would aid ministers to avoid "so much blundering."[42]

The emergence of the church in the North as a middle-class denomination was evinced also by the increasing

38 General Missionary Convention, *Report of the Proceedings of the Twenty-Third Anniversary Meeting* . . . (Cincinnati, 1871), 8.

39 "Pathfinder," *Christian Oracle*, IX (October 11, 1894), 596. See also "Our Budget," *Christian Evangelist*, XXXII (February 7, 1895), 84.

40 James Small, "A Visit in Iowa," *Christian Standard*, XXXIII (October 23, 1897), 1356.

41 [J. Z. Tyler], "Business in Religion," *Christian Examiner*, XII (June 13, 1879), 2.

42 G. L. Brokaw, "Iowa Notes and News," *Christian Evangelist*, XXI (January 25, 1894), 60.

activity of businessmen in church work. City ministers were urged to make use of the talents of the businessmen in their congregations since the wealthy were generally "good planners" and "hustlers."[43] By the 1890s most of the very wealthy men in the movement had been pushed into places of national prominence in various church organizations both because their "business sense" was "sorely needed" and because of their "ability to aid financially."[44]

During the same decades the economic thought of most Southern church leaders was running in entirely different channels. Conservative preachers attacked the "delusive idea of the overshadowing importance of the city churches" and insisted that the "best classes of people" lived in the rural areas.[45] "Great cities," stated a conservative Missouri magazine, "are the great corrupters of the morals of mankind, like lewd women."[46] Moses E. Lard, noted pioneer preacher in Kentucky and Missouri, conveniently summed up the ideals of the Southern church: "The preacher of that golden age was a farmer. . . . He geared his horse with dexterity, plowed with as much skill as ever did Lycurgus, and could whistle 'old Father Grimes' with an unction which will never be equaled by Bro. Moore's organist in Cincinnati."[47]

Southern church leaders frequently attacked "aristocrats" and what they thought were efforts by Northern churchmen to cater to the whims of the wealthy. In 1892, David Lipscomb was disturbed by plans to build a $30,000 church building in Atlanta and predicted that such "extravagance" would "weaken instead of strengthen them."[48] Fletcher D. Srygley,

---

[43] F. M. Cummings, "Business Men in the Sunday-School," *Christian Standard*, XXVI (May 30, 1891), 448.

[44] J. G. Waggoner, "Christian Business Men of Illinois," *ibid.*, XXV (July 19, 1890), 474.

[45] W. B. F. Treat, "Religion in the Cities," *American Christian Review*, XIX (November 12, 1878), 361. See also David Edwin Harrell, Jr., A Decade of Disciples of Christ Social Thought, 1875-1885 (unpublished M. A. thesis, Vanderbilt University, 1958), 45-87, and Harrell, Social History of the Disciples of Christ, 164-168.

[46] "Great Cities," *Christian Pioneer*, VII (August 1, 1867), 412.

[47] "Pioneer Preaching in the West," *Apostolic Times*, III (February 8, 1872), 348.

[48] "Fine Houses for Worship," *Gospel Advocate*, XXXIV (January 28, 1892), 52. See also "Miscellany," *ibid.*, XXXIV (April 21, 1892), 248.

the wit of the *Gospel Advocate*, wrote in 1891:

> The Northern Christian publishes an article from the Oregonian on "Why People Don't Go To Church." This reminds me that a friend of mine asked a highly respectable and strictly moral but irreligious man why he did not go to church, and the man said he stayed away from such places out of respect for his deceased old mother who was a deeply pious woman and who always taught him never to attend places of fashionable amusement on Sunday![49]

An editorial in the conservative *Octographic Review* clearly stated the anti-aristocratic prejudices of Southern preachers: "The perils of religion thus consist in wealth and ignorance. . . . Wealth brings luxury, worldliness, negligence. . . . Rich men in the church! Millionaires sons of God . . . ! Did godliness ever grow out of that kind of soil?"[50]

These diverging economic views were everywhere a part of the pattern of the dividing church. Conservative editors repeatedly charged Northern church periodicals with domination by aristocrats. An early biographer of Isaac Errett wrote: "In Cincinnati it was believed at the time, or at any rate it was so represented that the 'Standard's' quarters were most gorgeous; and the 'Review' had visions of Brussels carpets, luxurious chairs . . . in which the editor . . . reclined and smoked his fragrant Havana! . . . It would make the impression that the 'Review' was the paper of the *people*–the 'Standard' was that of a select aristocratic *class*."[51] By the late 1880s the *Christian Evangelist*, then the leading liberal journal in the church, was accused of making a "constant bid" for the support of the "rich, high-minded, and half-converted"

49 "From the Papers," *ibid.*, XXXIII (June 3, 1891), 338.

50 "The Chief Perils of Religion," *Octographic Review*, XXX (June 23, 1887), 4.

51 Lamar, *Memoirs of Errett*, I, 308.

and ignoring the poor.[52]

Southern preachers frequently linked their economic opinions with conservative theology in condemning such "liberal innovations" as instrumental music and missionary societies. The outspoken Texas conservative, Thomas R. Burnett, betrayed his bias against wealth and fashion in an 1895 attack on the Texas Missionary Society:

> Last week about a hundred preachers and fashionable women assembled at Gainesville, Texas, in a state convention, and wasted enough of the Lord's money and time to have held a hundred protracted meetings. . . . They also spent enough money for extra fine toggery, to appear in style, to pay the expenses of a half dozen evangelists to preach the gospel in destitute places all summer. What was their business at Gainesville? Principally a fashionable blow-out, and in addition to this, an effort to push forward the furor for societies and fads in religion, and to supplant the Lord's plan of work and worship in the churches.[53]

David Lipscomb surmised that the "fundamental difference between the Disciples of Christ [i.e. Churches of Christ] and the society folks" was that the conservatives wanted people "to come to Christ," while the liberals wanted to build "a strong and respectable denomination" based on "moneyed societies, fine houses, fashionable music, and eloquent speeches."[54]

One of the most perceptive nineteenth-century analyses of the sociological roots of the Disciples of Christ schism was

---

[52] "'The Great Robbery,'" *Octographic Review*, XXXI (July 12, 1888), 1. David Lipscomb believed that as a general rule the "working people" of the North had been "weaned from the church by the building and conducting of churches, suited in style, buildings, and worship for the rich." "A Visit to Chattanooga," *Gospel Advocate*, XXXI (April 3, 1889), 214.

[53] "Burnett's Budget," *ibid.*, XXXVII (July 4, 1895), 419.

[54] "The Churches Across the Mountains," *ibid.*, XXXIX (January 7, 1897), 4.

made by a conservative editor, Daniel Sommer. He wrote:

> As time advanced such of those churches as assembled in large towns and cities gradually became proud, or at least, sufficiently worldly-minded to desire popularity, and in order to attain that unscriptural end they adopted certain popular arrangements such as the hired pastor, the church choir, instrumental music, man-made societies to advance the gospel, and human devices to raise money to support previously mentioned devices of similar origin. In so doing they divided the brotherhood of disciples.[55]

While Sommer's charge that liberals were responsible for the schism is biased, and his judgments on what is "unscriptural" are open to question, his understanding of the relationship between economic and theological outlook is a rare piece of insight.

A recent historian of the Disciples of Christ, in evaluating one of the conservative periodicals of the post-Civil War period, wrote, "If one were hunting incidents to illustrate a thesis for a modern volume entitled 'The Social Sources of Denominationalism,' an excellent example could be presented in the reaction [to the founding of the *Christian Standard*] of the *American Christian Review*."[56] The *Review* does vividly show the relationship between religious faith and social force; but no more or less than every other Disciples periodical of the nineteenth century.[57] Conservative and liberal theological positions, Northern and Southern sectional feeling, urban and rural prejudices, and agricultural and middle-class economic views were all important ingredients in the nineteenth-century fracturing of the movement. Every

---

55 "Signs of the Times," *Octographic Review*, XI (October 25, 1897), 1.

56 Garrison and DeGroot, *Disciples of Christ*, 357.

57 The *Review* is certainly not unique. It is interesting that a liberal historian should see the sociological roots of the conservatives in the movement but fail to see that sectionalism and economics also played a part in the policy of Northern church papers.

Disciples periodical and every Disciples minister during these critical years represented not simply a theological position but a describable mixture of one or another of these clashing viewpoints. The twentieth-century Churches of Christ are the spirited offspring of the religious rednecks of the post bellum South.[58]

[58] Of course, the Churches of Christ have not remained an economic and cultural unit since 1906. The sociological and economic elevation of a portion of the membership of the church, especially since World War II, has motivated a large part of the church to begin the transition toward denominationalism. The result is that the movement is once again dividing along sociological lines. Conservative appeals in the movement in the 1960s have a distinctive lower class and anti-aristocratic flavor, while the centers of liberalism are in the areas where the church is most numerous and sophisticated.

# THE APOCALYPTIC ORIGINS OF CHURCHES OF CHRIST AND THE TRIUMPH OF MODERNISM

**Richard T. Hughes**

The origins of the American-born Churches of Christ are exceedingly complex. While most historians have argued that Churches of Christ separated from Alexander Campbell's Disciples of Christ late in the nineteenth century, this essay will suggest that the genesis of Churches of Christ was not a matter of separation from the Disciples at all. Rather, Churches of Christ grew from two early nineteenth-century worldviews that coalesced and intertwined with one another in ways that often defy disentanglement. The first was the apocalyptic perspective of Barton W. Stone; the second was the radically sectarian mentality of the young and brash Alexander Campbell of the *Christian Baptist* period (1823-1830). As early as the 1830s, these two perspectives wed, brought together in part by the matchmaking power of poverty, marginality, and social estrangement.[1] Together, they clearly shaped a portion of the Stone-Campbell movement

[1] Poverty was not the defining factor in the 1830s, but it was important. Later, in the South, the Civil War helped to enhance the sectarian outlook, as Professor David Edwin Harrell has amply documented. See Harrell, "The Sectional Origins of Churches of Christ," *Journal of Southern History* 30 (August 1964): 261-77.

that, in due time, would come to be known as a denomination separate from the Disciples; namely, the Churches of Christ.

While the perspectives of Stone and the early Campbell intertwined in the lives and thoughts of many in the early nineteenth century, and while the one rarely existed without the other, it is nonetheless possible to identify particular leaders and to discern particular streams of tradition that carried either the Stoneite or the early Campbellian perspective in especially powerful ways. Thus, for example, Campbell's sectarian perspective, which many of his early followers interpreted to mean that Churches of Christ constituted the one true church outside of which there was no salvation, fed through several influential editor-preachers. Most notable among these were Tolbert Fanning and John R. Howard of Tennessee, Arthur Crihfield of Ohio and Kentucky, and Benjamin Franklin and Daniel Sommer of Indiana.[2] Since this tradition is relatively well known, I will not trace it here.

This essay will focus, instead, on the worldview embraced by Barton W. Stone and the sizable corps of preachers he inspired in the Cumberland region of Tennessee in the early nineteenth century and on the ways in which that worldview helped define a sizable segment of Churches of Christ. This worldview could best be described, quite simply, as *apocalyptic*, embracing a radical sense of estrangement and separation from the world and its values and a keen allegiance to a transcendent vision these people described as "the Kingdom of God." That kingdom had manifested itself in the earliest days of primitive Christianity, perpetually stood in judgment on the kingdoms of this earth, and would finally triumph over all things. Because Stone and his people identified so strongly with that kingdom, they typically

---

[2] While Alexander Campbell never claimed, even during the *Christian Baptist* period, that the movement he led comprised the one and only true church, much of his early rhetoric pointed in that direction. By the late 1830s, Crihfield and Howard, in particular, were defending the Church of Christ as the one true Church. For Crihfield and Howard, see Richard T. Hughes and C. Leonard Allen, *Illusions of Innocence: Protestant Primitivism in America, 1630-1875* (Chicago: University of Chicago Press, 1988), 128-31.

refused to fight in wars, to vote, or otherwise to participate in the political process.

The apocalyptic worldview, however, should not be confused with premillennialism. There were those, as we shall see, who followed the apocalyptic perspective into a full-blown premillennial outlook. This, however, was not always the case. Indeed, on the Stone side of the movement, there were some who embraced the apocalyptic worldview but stoutly resisted premillennial thinking. On the Campbell side of the movement, there were some who arrived at premillennial convictions out of sheer biblical literalism with no reference whatever to what we here describe as an "apocalyptic worldview."

The irony here is that, while many in the movement uncritically fused the Stoneite and early Campbellian perspectives, in significant ways these perspectives were simply incompatible. For if Stone's worldview was predominantly apocalyptic, Campbell's outlook—even during the sectarian days of the *Christian Baptist*—was fundamentally optimistic regarding this world, progressive, and postmillennial. Further, the intellectual split between Campbell and Stone in this regard reflected a major split in American intellectual life at that time, the split between the "party of memory" and the "party of hope."

In the twentieth century, in the interest of modernization, key leaders of Churches of Christ literally drove from the church both the memory and the reality of the separationist and apocalyptic vision inspired by Barton W. Stone. Discredited and forgotten, this tradition therefore has played no meaningful role in the historiography of Churches of Christ.

## Historiography, Cultural Setting, and Backgrounds

In 1906, the United States Bureau of the Census recognized for the first time a division in the ranks of the Stone-Campbell restoration tradition and listed two separate denominations: Churches of Christ and Disciples of Christ. Until 1964, most historians rooted this division in a late nineteenth-century dispute over missionary societies and instrumental music in worship, with the emerging Churches of Christ coalescing around the negative position on both these issues. In this view, the Disciples represented the mainstream of this tradition throughout the nineteenth century and even into the twentieth. On the other hand, Churches of Christ departed from that mainstream, as well as from the parent denomination, the Disciples, over these issues and, therefore, possessed little theological identity apart from their resistance to these "innovations."[3]

However, in 1964, David Edwin Harrell took sharp exception to this interpretation and rooted the division in social forces related to the Civil War. Noting that Churches of Christ in the early twentieth century resided overwhelmingly in the upper South and that Disciples in the same period

---

[3] This historiographic perspective has been shaped chiefly by historians writing from within the Disciples of Christ side of this movement. See, e.g., W. E. Garrison and A. T. DeGroot, *The Disciples of Christ: A History* (St. Louis: Christian Board of Publication, 1948), 404-6; and William E. Tucker and Lester G. McAllister, *Journey in Faith: A History of the Christian Church (Disciples of Christ)* (St. Louis: Bethany Press, 1975), 251-54. Most major histories of American religion rely on precisely this interpretation. See, e.g., Sydney E. Ahlstrorn, *A Religious History of the American People* (New Haven: Yale University Press, 1972), 822-23; Edwin S. Gaustad, *A Religious History of America*, rev. ed. (San Francisco: Harper and Row, 1990), 258; and Winthrop S. Hudson, *Religion in America: An Historical Account of the Development of American Religious Life*, 4th ed. (New York: Macmillan, 1987), 260, n. 25. Interestingly, the only text to date whose chief interest is a synthetic history of Churches of Christ employs the same interpretive assumptions but for opposite purposes. Thus, Earl I. West argues that "by 1906, . . . the 'Christian Churches' or 'Disciples of Christ,' as they preferred to be called, took their instruments and their missionary societies and walked a new course." See *The Search for the Ancient Order*, 2 vols. (Indianapolis: Earl West Religious Book Service, 1950), 2:448.

centered in the Midwest, Harrell concluded that the genesis of Churches of Christ as a denomination separate from the Disciples must have been sectional. Thus, poverty versus affluence and rural versus urban biases, along with deep sectional feelings, were all tensions that divided the movement and helped produce Churches of Christ as a separate and distinct denomination. Thus, he concluded, "the twentieth-century Churches of Christ are the spirited offspring of the religious rednecks of the postbellum South."[4]

There is considerable truth both in the traditional reading and in Harrell's revisionist interpretation. At the same time, neither of these interpretations recognizes the pivotal role played by the separationist and apocalyptic tradition of Barton W. Stone in shaping Churches of Christ, much less the cultural split that undergirded the differences between the Campbellite and the Stoneite perspectives.

How might one describe that "cultural split"? On the one hand, the dominant outlook of antebellum America was a postmillennial perspective that celebrated unbounded human potential and unrestrained progress into the modern world. Those who held this viewpoint comprised the "party of hope," perhaps best epitomized by Ralph Waldo Emerson. Further, many who held this position were primitivists who took their bearings from a mythic, primordial age—a point underscored by Major L. Wilson in a seminal essay published in 1961. As Wilson put it, "the politics of restoration was not. . . a conservative flight to the past" but instead a vision of

4 Harrell, "Sectional Origins," 264, 277. See also David Edwin Harrell, *Quest for a Christian America: The Disciples of Christ and American Society to 1866* (Nashville: Disciples of Christ Historical Society, 1966); and David Edwin Harrell, *The Social Sources of Division in the Disciples of Christ, 1865-1900* (Atlanta: Publishing Systems, Inc., 1973). Bill J. Humble shared the view that the Civil War, with its attendant social factors, played a significant role in dividing the Disciples into two separate communions. See B. J. Humble, "The Influence of the Civil War," *Restoration Quarterly* 8 (Fourth Quarter 1965): 245.

primordial perfections that "made further progress possible."[5] Those who took this view were confident that, through their own efforts, they could recover the perfections of that primal age and project those perfections into the American future. They would therefore recreate, in their own time, the kingdom of God on earth.[6]

Those Americans who embraced the minority position, on the other hand, placed themselves in radical opposition to this perspective and generally affirmed a pessimistic and anti-modern worldview that frequently turned out to be profoundly apocalyptic. Often Calvinists convinced of the radical sinfulness of humankind, these Americans comprised the "party of memory" of which Emerson so loudly complained. Many of these also were primitivists, but their skepticism regarding human potential and progress prevented them from easily projecting the perfections of the first age into an American future. Instead, these Americans often proclaimed their allegiance to a "kingdom of God" which they saw manifest in the primordium and which they anticipated would manifest itself again in the millennium, but only at God's initiative. They simply had no confidence that the kingdom of God could appear between those end times of

---

[5] Major L. Wilson, "Paradox Lost: Order and Progress in Evangelical Thought of Mid-Nineteenth-Century America," *Church History* 44 (September 1975): 352-54. R. W. B. Lewis made the same point when he argued that "the more intense the belief in progress toward perfection, the more it stimulated a belief in a present primal perfection." See *The American Adam: Innocence, Tragedy, and Tradition in the Nineteenth Century* (Chicago: University of Chicago Press, 1955), 5. Richard Hofstadter concurred in *The Progressive Historians: Turner, Beard, Parrington* (New York: Vintage Books, 1970), 7, arguing that American progress often was progress backward to "the primitivist sense of the ideal human condition." There was by no means consensus in antebellum America on the specific content of the primordial age.

[6] Clearly, many of the Transcendentalist communal experiments reflected this outlook. Thus, Bronson Alcott saw America as the site of "the second Eden" in which humankind might be restored to "rightful communion with God in the Paradise of Good." See Clara E. Sears, *Bronson Alcott's Fruitlands, with Transcendental Wild Oats by Louisa Alcott* (Boston: Houghton Mifflin, 1915). John Humphrey Noyes imagined that the millennial age in which he lived, patterned after the perfections of the primitive church, would sustain not only social relationships free from selfish pride but even the scientific breeding of the perfect human being. See Maren Lockwood Carden, *Oneida: Utopian Community to Modern Corporation* (Baltimore: Johns Hopkins University Press, 1969; repr., New York: Harper and Row, 1971), 12-13. Similarly, the humanitarian crusade aimed at nothing less than the complete elimination of evil from the social fabric of American life.

God-directed, primal perfections. For these Americans, primitivism often took on distinctly anti-modern dimensions.[7]

The division that finally produced Disciples of Christ on the one hand and Churches of Christ on the other, while rooted in a variety of factors, had its oldest and deepest roots in this ideological polarization. Indeed, the Disciples of Christ are the legitimate children of the postmillennial, modernizing progressivism of the mature Alexander Campbell—a man who represented the "party of hope" as fully as any man of his age. Churches of Christ, on the other hand, ultimately descend, at least in part, from the separatist, anti-modern perspective of Barton W. Stone, who stood squarely in the "party of memory."[8]

Yet, it must be said that for all their mutual enmity, the party of hope and the party of memory shared significant common ground. The fact that nineteenth-century Americans often rooted progress in the perfections of the primal past helps us understand how the Campbell and Stone movements, embracing as they did such radically differing worldviews, could unite in 1832. Indeed, most in both groups were convinced that they shared common restorationist presuppositions. How different those presuppositions really were became evident as the nineteenth century wore on, slowly revealing the existence of two denominations, not one: the Disciples and the Churches of Christ.

Indeed, recognition of these two divergent traditions helps account for the North/South sectional alignment of Disciples

---

[7] Why, in an age dominated by postmillennial dreams and anticipations, would this minority voice exist at all? In the first place, Calvinism—with its emphasis on the sovereignty of God and the fallenness of humankind—led some to view with profound suspicion the assumption that human beings might create, through their own efforts, the kingdom of God on earth. In the second place, many who embraced such skepticism were people estranged from the progress and optimism of the age by social and economic circumstances. Thus, many found in William Miller's prediction that Christ would return in 1843 meaningful compensation for economic losses occasioned by the depression of 1837.

[8] Almost alone among historians, Martin Marty recognized that the division between Disciples and Churches of Christ was finally a division between modernism and primitivism. See *Modern American Religion*, vol. 1: *The Irony of It All, 1893-1919* (Chicago: University of Chicago Press, 1986), 163-64. Marty's account does not recognize, however, that this ideological split was rooted in the differing worldviews of Alexander Campbell and Barton W. Stone.

and Churches of Christ. While Professor Harrell's "sectional origins" thesis helps account to a great degree for the sectional alignment of these traditions, that thesis still leaves much unexplained.[9] In the first place, if the identity of Churches of Christ was principally defined by southern sectional prejudices, why did these churches thrive only in a relatively small region of the South—in Tennessee, southern Kentucky, and northern Alabama, but hardly at all in the deep South and the Southeast? Even more important, when the two major terms of the Stone-Campbell movement's agenda—unity and restoration—finally broke apart, why did the restoration ideal make its home chiefly among Churches of Christ in the upper South, while the unity theme made its home chiefly among Disciples in the Middle West?

On the other hand, taking seriously the differences between Stone and the mature Campbell helps clarify answers to these questions. From the earliest years of the nineteenth century, a major strand of the movement that would become Churches of Christ centered in the Cumberland Plateau of Tennessee, an area where the leadership of Barton W. Stone was pronounced. R. L. Roberts, in fact, has compiled a list of approximately 200 preachers in the Cumberland area, all influenced either directly or indirectly by Barton W. Stone, who were actively establishing Churches of Christ long before the mid-1820s when Campbell was first known in that region. From that time on, Campbell made occasional visits to middle Tennessee, but he preached mainly in cities and towns, leaving the sizable corps of Stoneite preachers to dominate the rural countryside.[10]

---

[9] Professor Harrell does speak of the "divided mind" of the movement. Thus, he writes:

> Two distinct emphases emerged. One group conceived of Christianity in the denominational framework of practical religion, social and political activism, and, often, a nationalistic postmillennialism. A second group emphasized the sectarian tradition of biblical legalism, a fanatical disposition, and uncompromising separation from the world. (*Quest for a Christian America*, 66.)

However, Harrell does not recognize that, among the various roots of the sectarian side of the movement, the Stoneite tradition played a prominent role, nor does he emphasize the apocalyptic dimensions that often accompanied the sectarian phase of the movement, especially in the South.

[10] R. L. Roberts, "Early Tennessee and Kentucky Preachers," unpublished paper.

On the other hand, Campbell's visits to Kentucky—an early bastion of the Stone movement—were far more frequent than his visits to Tennessee, and his long-term influence centered, therefore, especially in Kentucky and points further north. It is hardly any wonder, then, that the strength of Disciples of Christ is especially pronounced to this day in the original Campbell heartland of Kentucky and the Middle West, while Churches of Christ find their greatest strength in the region bounded by the Cumberland Plateau on the east and Texas on the west.[11]

The story that follows is one of competing perspectives on the value of this world, human progress, and modernity. The story concludes, however, with profound irony, for while Campbell's early, sectarian view of both church and Scripture dominated Churches of Christ from the 1820s on, his optimistic assessment of this world and of human progress finally came to dominate them as well. This was a slow development, gathering momentum for over 100 years. Finally, in the World War I era, Churches of Christ took a decisive turn away from the old Stoneite worldview, increasingly embracing Campbell's optimistic assessment of human progress. As a result, these churches became agents of modernization as fully as did Campbell's Disciples; the primitivism of Churches of Christ became, not a foe of modernization, but a pivotal support for that process; and the traditional Stoneite insistence on separation from the world finally became little more than sectarian exclusivism, calling only for separation from the surrounding denominations.

---

[11] For delineation of the sectional alignments of Disciples and Churches of Christ in 1906, see Harrell, "Sectional Origins," 263-64. By 1950, Disciples of Christ had their greatest strength in the five states comprising the original Campbell heartland—Kentucky, Ohio, Indiana, Illinois, and Missouri—and in Texas, with slightly lesser strength in Iowa, Kansas, and Oklahoma to the west and in Virginia and North Carolina to the east. See Edwin S. Gaustad, *Historical Atlas of Religion in America* (New York: Harper and Row, 1962), 65. On the other hand, by 1960, Churches of Christ were especially concentrated in middle and western Tennessee, northern Alabama, Arkansas, Oklahoma, and Texas. See Edwin S. Gaustad, "Churches of Christ in America," in *The Religious Situation: 1969*, ed. Donald R. Cutler (Boston: Beacon Press, 1969), 1030-31. Both Disciples and Churches of Christ by the mid-twentieth century had significant strength in southern California, a phenomenon explained by westward migration patterns.

## Alexander Campbell

Alexander Campbell exerted little or no influence on the sizable Stoneite communities of Kentucky, southern Ohio, and middle Tennessee—communities most often called Churches of Christ—until 1823, when he traveled to Kentucky to debate William L. McCalla. The Stoneites, whose insistence on Christian freedom had left them almost vacuous theologically, found compelling Campbell's clear and detailed exposition of the forms, structures, and practices of primitive Christianity.[12] From that time on, Campbell exercised a growing, and finally decisive, influence over Churches of Christ in that region. Indeed, in January 1832, the Stone and Campbell movements formally united in Lexington, Kentucky.[13]

For almost a decade prior to that union, Campbell had contributed to Churches of Christ a Common Sense view of the Bible drawn directly from Scottish Baconianism,[14] a clear and detailed description of those aspects of the primitive church that ought to be restored, and great confidence that human beings were fully capable of reading Scripture aright, implementing its divine patterns, and restoring in full the grandeur and beauty of the apostolic age.

Campbell's great confidence in human insight and human ability to bring about moral and spiritual reform stood at the intellectual heart of his movement and, more than anything else, distinguished his movement from that of Barton W. Stone. But Campbell also differed from Stone in his understanding of Christian primitivism. For this reason, Campbell's position can be designated "rational, progressive primitivism." Indeed, restoration for Campbell was not so much a response to the sovereign rule of God, understood in

[12] See Hughes and Allen, *Illusions of Innocence*, 115-16.

[13] See Dean Mills, *Union on the King's Highway: The Campbell-Stone Heritage of Unity* (Joplin, Mo.: College Press, 1987).

[14] See Samuel Morris Eames, *The Philosophy of Alexander Campbell* (Bethany, W.Va.: Bethany College, 1966), esp. 19-32; and Robert F. West, *Alexander Campbell and Natural Religion* (New Haven: Yale University Press, 1948), 220-21, 225.

Calvinist terms, as it was a response to the authority of Scripture, understood in some respects as a technical, even scientific, manual for the recovery of primitive Christianity. Clearly, Enlightenment perspectives significantly shaped Campbell's restoration vision which, when all was said and done, focused on *progress toward* the rule of God, aided by rational analysis and technical reconstruction of the first Christian age. Ultimately, a complete restoration of the apostolic institutions would transform human society and launch the millennial dawn.[15]

However, Campbell also was convinced that the millennium would be the fruit of rational and scientific progress and simply would not—and could not—begin until scientific progress had run its course, enlightening all humankind. He made this point abundantly clear in 1858 in response to claims that the revival of that year was the harbinger of the golden age. In rebutting this claim, Campbell argued for the following "incomparably paramount" consideration:

> It was but yesterday that the mariner's compass was discovered, that printing was shown to be practicable, that steam power was laughed at as an absurdity, and the electric telegraph ridiculed as the hobby of a vagarian's brain. . . . We have too much faith in progress . . . to subscribe to the doctrines of these theological gentlemen who hint the last days are at hand."[16]

But there was no exchange that more clearly illumined Campbell's postmillennial principles than his quarrel in 1833-34 with Samuel M. McCorkle. Profoundly pessimistic

15 On Campbell's postmillennialism, see West, *Alexander Campbell and Natural Religion*, 163-217; and Carl Wayne Hensley, "The Rhetorical Vision of the Disciples of Christ: A Rhetoric of American Millennialism" (Ph.D. diss., University of Minnesota, 1972).

16 Campbell, "The Millennium," *Millennial Harbinger* (hereafter MH), 5th series, 1 (June 1858): 335-36.

about human progress, McCorkle challenged Campbell's most fundamental presupposition regarding the possibility of recovering a golden age. "The present cannot be renovated," McCorkle complained. "No means on earth can bring or restore the administration back to primitive rectitude; it grows worse yearly in despite of all the efforts that can be made to heal."[17] Writing under the pseudonym "A Reformed Clergyman," Campbell was incredulous. Had not Bacon, Locke, and Newton inspired tremendous progress in politics and science? And what of the noble contributions of Luther, Calvin, and Zwingli? Beyond this, "the invention of gunpowder, the mariner's compass, the printing press, the discovery of America, the American Revolution—what have they wrought!!" Even Campbell's own movement might well launch "a restoration" that would "bless the world in ten thousand ways." A millennium would dawn, to be sure, and its driving force would be "knowledge, scientific, political, and religious."[18] To Campbell, the conclusion of the entire matter was clear:

> This is, of all ages and of all generations, the most unpropitious for the assertion of the dogma that moral and intellectual means can benefit society in no very valuable nor permanent way. Almost every common newspaper presents insuperable difficulties to such a preposterous opinion.[19]

By 1844, McCorkle found refuge not in Campbell's *Millennial Harbinger* but in Barton W. Stone's *Christian Messenger*. Indeed, Stone opened to McCorkle the pages of the *Messenger* for a lengthy series of articles in which

[17] S. M. McCorkle, "Signs of the Times," MH 4 (October 1833): 483.

[18] A Reformed Clergyman, "The Millennium—No. 3," MH 5 (October 1834): 549; "The Millennium—No. 7," MH 6 (March 1835): 105; and "The Millennium—No. 8," MH 6 (April 1835): 148.

[19] A Reformed Clergyman, "The Millennium—No. 3," MH 5 (October 1834): 549-50.

McCorkle launched a massive counterattack on Campbell's views." '*Restoration of ancient order*,' is a pleasing *dream*—a brilliant phantom," McCorkle began in July, and he specifically called on Campbell to show how the "man of sin" might be destroyed by merely "moral means." By August, McCorkle took the gloves off and came out swinging.

> Great names in the Christian church have vetoed the doctrine of a personal reign of Messiah, and our credulous brethren following in the perilous *wake*! . . . Half inebriate with the *fumes* of Babylon, . . . [editors] are harping upon, "Christianity restored," when we are Approaching a *time of trouble*, such as never was. . . . Will they counteract by the "Ancient Order" the strong delusion that God has promised to send. . .?[20]

## Barton W. Stone

It is significant that McCorkle chose to publish these strictures in Stone's *Christian Messenger* and that Stone chose to print them. Perhaps even more significant is McCorkle's confession to Stone: "With the exception of yourself, I have the editorial corps [of the movement] against me."[21] While Stone did not approve of all that McCorkle wrote, he was profoundly sympathetic with McCorkle's pessimistic outlook on human potential and progress. Indeed, in spite of their rejection of Calvinist theories of conversion, Stone and his followers—most of whom came from Presbyterian or Baptist backgrounds—continued to nurture for many years a Calvinist assessment of human nature.[22]

---

[20] S. M. McCorkle, "Conversion of the World, No. 4," *Christian Messenger* (hereafter CM) 14 (July 1844): 70-71; and "Conversion of the World—No. 4 [*sic*]," CM 14 (August 1844): 97-98.

[21] S. M. McCorkle, "The Laymen [*sic*]," CM 13 (March 1844): 349.

[22] See Newell D. Williams, "Barton W. Stone's Calvinist Piety," *Encounter* 42 (Autumn 1981): 409-17; and Hughes and Allen, *Illusions of Innocence*, 112-16.

Stone typified most when he wrote:

> That mankind are depraved, is a lamentable truth, abundantly attested by the word of God, and confirmed by universal experience and observation. . . . All are in want of what they were made to enjoy, which is God; and have a propensity to satisfy that want with meaner things.[23]

Stone's followers generally joined to their Calvinist appraisal of human nature an experience of poverty and deprivation. John Rogers, one of the early Stone preachers in Kentucky, later recalled that the pioneers "were mostly men of small means" who "knew nothing of the luxuries and refinements of modern society." Isaac Jones recalled that all the preachers in middle Tennessee and south central Kentucky early on were "poor men, (some having no homes of their own) having but little education. . . ."[24] While Campbell preached in meeting houses, Stone's early preaching is described as largely itinerant, being "done under an Elm and Oak" and "under a Beech Tree, covered with a summer grapevine." And if Campbell moved among the cultured and the sophisticated, the work of Stone and his colleagues was among rustic and unlettered frontier people whose religious practices were often both primitive and emotional.[25] Further, the Stoneites typically idealized poverty as a Christian virtue—a fact that stands in stark contrast to Alexander Campbell, who died the wealthiest man in West Virginia, having plowed an inheritance from his father-in-law

[23] B. W. Stone, "A Compendious View of the Gospel," in *The Biography of Eld. Barton Warren Stone, Written by Himself* (Cincinnati, 1847), repr. in Hoke S. Dickinson, ed., *The Cane Ridge Reader* (Paris, Ky.: Cane Ridge Preservation Project, 1972), 191-92.

[24] John Rogers, "Funeral Discourse on Elder H. Dinsmore," *American Christian Review* 6 (September 17, 1863): 181; and Isaac N. Jones, "The Reformation in Tennessee," included in J. W. Grant, "A Sketch of the Reformation in Tennessee," c. 1897, typescript, 35 (manuscript housed in Center for Restoration Studies, Abilene Christian University).

[25] Grant, "A Sketch of the Reformation in Tennessee," 9-10; cf. Jones, "The Reformation in Tennessee," 31-32; and Joseph Thomas, *The Life of the Pilgrim Joseph Thomas* (Winchester, Va., 1817), 124, 160, 162-63, and *passim*.

into farming, land speculation, book publishing, and educational enterprises.

Finally, the Stoneites were every bit as utopian and restorationist as Alexander Campbell, but for them, restoration had less to do with the forms and structures of the primitive church and more to do with lives of simple holiness.

These features, taken together, nurtured in Stone and his people a distinctly anti-modern bias and helped sustain their apocalyptic outlook. That outlook, in turn, expressed itself in three specific ways: their insistence on a radical separation from the world; an eschatology that often manifested itself in premillennial terms; and their disdain for political involvement of any kind.

The theme of separation from the world abounds on almost every page of fourteen volumes of Stone's *Christian Messenger*, which ran from 1827 through 1844. Stone himself is a case in point. Aiming originally at a career in law, Stone abandoned that for a career in preaching. Then, when he and four other dissidents left the Presbyterian church in the aftermath of the Cane Ridge Revival, Stone voluntarily relinquished all salary and committed himself to a life of poverty in the interest of the kingdom of God. If Stone had a creed, he surely expressed it in 1841 when he admonished his readers "that you must not mind earthly things, nor set your affections on them—not to be conformed to the world. . . . Here you have no abiding place, but are as strangers and pilgrims seeking a better country."[26]

All of this stands in remarkable contrast to the world Martha Wilson, a mountain girl from North Carolina, found at Campbell's Bethany College in 1858. Having accompanied her husband to Bethany, Martha wrote home to her Aunt Julia in Yadkinville that she and Virgil, her husband, had "had invitations to tea at Mr. Campbell's and most of the *Professors*. They are all very sociable and friendly but there are rather more grades and circles in society than I think ought to be in a Christian community." In another letter, she complained, "I do not like to visit here—the people visit too

[26] Stone, *Biography*, 49-50; and "Christian Union. Lecture III," CM 11 (May 1841): 316-17.

fashionably." Yet, her husband was awed with the prospects facing Bethany graduates. He wrote, "Tell Uncle that a great many young men go out from college to teach, but owing to the reputation of Bethany for its instruction, they command enormous prices never less than $800. One young preacher has been offered $1500 in S. Virginia to preach for three churches."[27] Without a doubt, the issue of orientation toward the world was a clear line of demarcation that separated the basic worldviews of the Stone and Campbell movements.

The Stoneites' radical sense of separation from the world grew quite naturally from their apocalyptic orientation—an outlook that often gave expression to an explicitly premillennial eschatology. Indeed, millennial excitement was central to the Stone movement from its inception at the Cane Ridge Revival of 1801. John Dunlavy recalled after the revival that many thought "the day of the Lord, or Millennium, was at hand, and that that revival would never cease until that day should commence." Levi Purviance remembered that, during the revivals, "many were fully persuaded that the glorious Millennial Day had commenced, and that the world would soon become the Kingdom of our Lord Jesus Christ."[28]

Due to paucity of sources, however, it is difficult to trace the progress of Stone's millennial thought between the revivals and 1827, when he launched the *Christian Messenger*. However, by the early 1830s, no one could doubt

---

[27] Letter from Martha Wilson to Aunt Julia, Bethany, Virginia, July 21, 1858, in Jones Family Papers, Southern Historical Collection, Wilson Library, University of North Carolina, Chapel Hill; Letter from Martha Wilson to Aunt Julia, Bethany, Virginia, September 11, 1858; and postscript to letter from Martha Wilson to Aunt Julia, Bethany, Virginia, July 21, 1858.

[28] John Dunlavy, *The Manifesto, or a Declaration of the Doctrine and Practice of the Church of Christ* (New York, 1847), 437; and Levi Purviance, *The Biography of Elder David Purviance* (Dayton, Ohio, 1848), ,248-49. See also B. W. Stone and others, *Observations on Church Government, By the Presbytery of Springfield,* 1808, in Dickinson,*The Cane Ridge Reader*, 12.

where he stood on the millennial question. One sample of his thinking—a reply to the Elder William Caldwell—will suffice.

> The second coming of Christ is at the commencement of his millennial reign on earth—here on earth he will reign till the 1000 years be finished—nor will he cease to reign on earth till he has raised from death the wicked, and judged them according to their works.[29]

While the Millerite excitement of the early 1840s exacerbated Stone's interest in this theme,[30] his convictions regarding the premillennial kingdom of Christ predated those events by many years.

It is precisely here, tucked away in the union of separationism and apocalypticism, that one finds the origin of a third theme central both to Stone and to a major stream in Churches of Christ for over a century. This tradition held that civil government—including American democracy—was both demonic and illegitimate and that Christians should refuse all active participation in government and politics, including voting. In fact, the Stoneites generally thought, following Daniel's vision in the second chapter of Daniel, that the kingdom of Christ would, in the last days, fill the entire earth, destroy every human government—democracies along with monarchies—and rule the earth along with Christ for a

---

[29] B. W. Stone, "To Elder William Caldwell," CM 8 (May 1834): 148; see also B. W. Stone, "The Millennium," CM 7 (October 1833): 314; and B. W. Stone, "Reply," CM 7 (December 1833): 365-66.

[30] See B. W. Stone, "The Signs of the Last Days," CM 12 (August 1842): 301-6; B. W. Stone, "Signs of the Last Days—continued," CM 12 (October 1842): 363-67; and B. W. Stone, "The Coming of the Son of God," CM 12 (April 1842): 166-70.

thousand years. Once again, Stone is a case in point:

> The lawful King, Jesus Christ, will shortly put them [human governments] all down, and reign with his Saints on earth a thousand years, without a rival. . . . Then shall all man made laws and governments be burnt up forever. These are the seat of the beast. . . . We must cease to support any other government on earth by our counsels, co-operation, and choice.[31]

Based on this fundamental presupposition, the Stoneites time and again admonished one another to total noninvolvement in civil government other than paying taxes and obeying civil law—but only those laws that did not conflict with the kingdom of God.[32]

In this connection, it should be noted that the Stoneites' rejection of ecclesiastical societies (missionary, Bible, temperance, etc.) grew out of the same apocalyptic vision that governed their refusal to participate in civil government. God had ordained none of these societies, and his coming kingdom would destroy them, along with all human governments and institutions devised by men's wits. On this point, the Stoneites stood once again in marked contrast with the Campbell movement. Campbell also stood opposed to ecclesiastical societies during the early years of his career, but he based his opposition not on apocalypticism but on the biblical pattern.

---

[31] B. W. S., "Reflections of Old Age," CM 13 (August 1843): 123-26. See also B. W. Stone, "Civil and Military Offices Sought and Held by Christians," CM 12 (May 1842): 201-5; letter to T. P. Ware and letter from T. P. Ware, CM 14 (October 1844): 163-71; and "An Interview Between an Old and Young Preacher," CM 14 (December 1844): 225-300.

[32] See James M. Mathes, "Number III," CM 10 (May 1836): 65-66; and Jn. T. Jones, Jno. Rigdon, M. Elder, and D. P. Henderson, Committee, "Report," CM 9 (November 1835): 250-51.

Further, Campbell abandoned his opposition in the 1840s and became president both of the American Christian Bible Society (1845) and the American Christian Missionary Society (1849).

Finally, since Daniel, chapter two, was such an important text for the apocalyptic visions of Stone and his people, it is interesting to note that Campbell tamed that passage and placed its meaning squarely in the context of human history and progress. For Campbell, the little stone that would fill the entire earth was not the coming kingdom of God but rather the Protestant Reformation, and the image that the stone destroyed was not human government but the Roman Catholic church.[33]

The contrast between Campbell and Stone with reference to the restoration vision can now be sharpened. If Campbell's vision can be called "rational, progressive primitivism," it is equally proper to name Stone's vision "apocalyptic primitivism." This designation points to his apocalyptic worldview which undergirded and sustained his premillennial perspective and which, in turn, reflected his Calvinist sense of the sovereignty of God. This meant that Stone was not so much interested in the church as in the *kingdom*, that is, the rule of God over all human affairs. That rule, he felt, was manifest preeminently in the restored church but would be consummated only in the premillennial second coming of Jesus Christ. Between the times, Stone felt, the kingdom of God was a countercultural reality that stood in judgment on all rational, scientific, and technical progress

[33] Alexander Campbell, "American Christian Missionary Society. President's Address," MH, 4th series, 2 (March 1852): 124.

and, indeed, on all human creations whatsoever.[34] More than anything else, this conviction formed the basis for Stone's anti-modern bias. Further, this apocalyptic and countercultural perspective provided the mainspring not only for Stone but also for a sizable segment of Churches of Christ until well into the twentieth century, even when that mainspring joined itself to the biblicism of Alexander Campbell.

## David Lipscomb

The man who more than anyone else carried this tradition into the twentieth century was David Lipscomb. Clearly the most influential person among Churches of Christ from the close of the Civil War until his death in 1917, Lipscomb edited the immensely influential *Gospel Advocate*, based in Nashville, Tennessee, for most of those years.

There is no question that Lipscomb was, in many ways, a Campbellite, holding a profoundly rational view of Scripture and even turning Campbell's biblicism toward legalism. As editor of the *Advocate*, Lipscomb inevitably stood at the heart of the fights between Churches of Christ and Disciples of Christ over missionary societies, the propriety of instrumental

[34] Most contemporary historians have not come to grips with the profound difference between Stone and Campbell regarding the restoration ideal. This is not surprising, for they also have failed to take seriously the apocalyptic worldview of Stone. David Edwin Harrell's work is a case in point. Harrell argued that Stone and Campbell alike were committed to a "spirit of moderation" and to postmillennial visions of social progress. Harrell, *Quest for a Christian America*, 36, 41, 45. Indeed, "prior to 1830, both [men] . . . linked their religious reform efforts with the eventual spiritual and social regeneration of the world." Interestingly, the one passage from Stone that Harrell cited to support this claim finds Stone arguing just the reverse, vehemently criticizing the postmillennial vision, and contending that "God would *overturn, and overturn, and overturn,* till Messiah shall reign alone, and all submit to his government." Harrell, *Quest for a Christian America*, 41. The passage Harrell cites from Stone is from "Remarks on Liberty of Conscience," CM 3 (February 1829): 91. Harrell did recognize that "the sectarian emphasis of nonparticipation in civil government centered around the influence of Barton Stone in the early years of the church," but he never connected that emphasis either with Stone's apocalyptic, countercultural worldview or with the very same perspective one finds later in both Tolbert Fanning and David Lipscomb. Harrell, *Quest for a Christian America*, 54-55.

music in worship, the role of women in the church, and basic attitudes toward Scripture. Further, it was Lipscomb who responded to S. N. D. North, director of the federal census of 1906, who thought he detected a major rupture in the Stone-Campbell movement. North was right, Lipscomb responded, and he urged him to list Churches of Christ completely separate from Disciples of Christ.[35]

Yet, if Lipscomb was a Campbellite who turned Campbell's own biblicism toward legalism, he also stood squarely and profoundly in the Stone tradition of separationism, apocalypticism, and apoliticism. It is difficult, if not impossible, to know all the sources for this emphasis in Lipscomb's thought. Given the pervasiveness of the Stone movement in middle Tennessee, Lipscomb could have been influenced by any one or combination of a number of Stoneite preachers. Undoubtedly, however, the critical link between Stone, a first generation leader, and Lipscomb, a third generation leader, was Tolbert Fanning, founding editor of several journals, including the *Gospel Advocate,* and the most powerful second-generation leader among mid-South Churches of Christ. He was also mentor to David Lipscomb. Fanning had been deeply influenced in his youth by three Stoneite preachers in northern Alabama: Ephraim D. Moore, James E. Matthews, and Ross Houston. From these men, especially Ephraim D. Moore, Fanning learned that "the Church of God is . . . destined, finally, . . . to triumph over all the powers of the earth."[36]

While apocalyptic in his thinking, however, Fanning was not premillennial. He did not expect the literal rule of Jesus

---

[35] David Lipscomb, "The 'Church of Christ' and the 'Disciples of Christ,'" *Gospel Advocate* (hereafter GA) 49 (July 18, 1907): 457.

[36] On Fanning, see James R. Wilburn, *The Hazard of the Die: Tolbert Fanning and the Restoration Movement* (Austin, Tex.: Sweet Publishing, 1969; repr., Malibu, Calif.: Pepperdine University Press, 1980). On Fanning's debt to Moore, Matthews, and Houston, see Wilburn, *Hazard*, 13-16; and Tolbert Fanning, "Obituary," GA 6 (January 1860): 31. On Fanning's early apocalypticism, see Tolbert Fanning, "Ministers of Peace in the World's Conflicts," GA 7 (November 1861): 347-48.

on this earth, nor did he expect any sort of divine rule for a literal thousand years. Nonetheless, he did expect God's rule to be realized on this earth when the kingdom of God would finally triumph over the kingdoms of this world. Accordingly, Fanning—like Stone before him—advised his people not to vote and espoused a consistently pacifist position.[37]

However, Fanning's apocalyptic worldview was different from that of Stone in other ways, for Fanning had absorbed the rational and technical perspectives of Campbell in a way that Stone had not. The kingdom of God remained for Stone a transcendent reality, never fully actualized in the present world, always standing in judgment of human creations and institutions, and destined to be realized completely in this world only at the end of time. Fanning's extreme Common Sense rationalism, however, led him to particularize the transcendent in ways that had been foreign to Stone. In Fanning's view, the kingdom of God was, in fact, the Church of Christ of his own temporal experience in Tennessee and the mid-South, and he wrote numerous articles explaining and defending this church to outsiders.[38]

The countercultural dimensions of Stone, therefore, while still alive in Fanning at one level, gave way at another level to sectarian exclusivism. Indeed, while it may appear that the increasingly dominant influence of Alexander Campbell in the Cumberland region simply obscured the old Stoneite worldview, this is not the case. Instead, Tolbert Fanning and his comrades, beginning in the late 1830s and 1840s, reshaped the Stoneite vision to make it more compatible with the sectarian vision of the early Alexander Campbell. Separation from the world, therefore, increasingly came to

[37] See Tolbert Fanning, "Reply to Brethren Lillard, Harding, and Ransome," GA 7 (September 1861): 265-76; "The Church of Christ in Prophecy No. 2," *Religious Historian* 2 (February 1873): 40-44; "Political Strife Amongst Christians," *Christian Review* 1 (August 1844): 184-85; "'The Kingdom of Heaven' A Spiritual Empire," *Christian Review* 3 (May 1846): 101; and "Peace," *Christian Review* 3 (March 1846): 65.

[38] Fanning, for example, ran an entire series of fourteen articles entitled simiply "The Church of Christ" in the *Gospel Advocate* from October 1855 through December 1856.

mean for Fanning and many of his generation simply opposition to the surrounding denominations.[39] For the remainder of the nineteenth century, more and more members of Churches of Christ conformed themselves to this sectarian understanding, lost their apocalyptic orientation, and reconciled themselves to participation in the American political system. In this way, Fanning helped subvert the anti-modern impulse in Stone and opened the way for the full-blown acceptance of modernity and modernization that would occur among Churches of Christ in the early twentieth century.

There were some, however, who kept alive the original Stoneite vision, and none were more important in this regard than David Lipscomb. In part because he had been mentored by Tolbert Fanning, Lipscomb stood squarely in the two worlds of Alexander Campbell and Barton Stone. He therefore embraced in his own person both the drive toward modernization and a distinctly anti-modern impulse.

Nonetheless, his success in combining the Campbell and Stone perspectives into a single outlook is a major reason for his tremendous power and influence throughout the increasingly heterogeneous fellowship of Churches of Christ. Had Lipscomb focused exclusively on the rational and legal side of Alexander Campbell, he would have alienated those whose roots ran deeply into the separationist piety of Barton Stone. And had Lipscomb focused only on the apocalyptic, separationist heritage of Stone, he would have alienated the legalists whose roots reached into the rationalism and biblicism of Campbell. Lipscomb's genius lay in the way he coherently combined these two perspectives into one. Further, Lipscomb was the last major leader in the history of Churches of Christ to combine these two perspectives successfully.

---

39 Most notable among Fanning's colleagues in the 1840s who employed an apocalyptic worldview to undergird their sectarian exclusivism were Arthur Crihfield and John R. Howard. On both, see Hughes and Allen, *Illusions of Innocence*, 128-31.

Following his death in 1917, the mainstream of Churches of Christ increasingly relegated the apocalyptic and anti-modern perspectives of the Stone movement to the status of heresy and built their house instead on the world-affirming foundation laid by Alexander Campbell, buttressed by the rational, legal, and technical themes that grew from Campbell's biblicism. Lipscomb stands, therefore, as a pinnacle in the history of Churches of Christ, looking backward to both Stone and Campbell and forward to a monolithic Church of Christ that would expel Stone's apocalyptic anti-modernism from its agenda.

Nonetheless, in his lifetime, Lipscomb was an articulate proponent of the Stoneite worldview. In the years immediately following the Civil War, Lipscomb published a series of articles on the Christian's relation to the world and especially to civil government and, in 1889, gathered these articles into a small book that received wide circulation among Churches of Christ. He called the book *Civil Government*, and a year after its publication he judged that "nothing we ever wrote so nearly affects the vital interests of the church of Christ and the salvation of the world as this little book."[40]

Lipscomb began with the Stoneite conviction that the Christian belongs to a kingdom ruled by God, not to the kingdoms ruled by humankind.[41] From this basic premise flowed the same themes that had characterized Stone: separation from the world, apocalypticism, and apoliticism.

Separation from the world meant for Lipscomb, first of all, reliance on the sovereign power of God. It was here that he found human institutions so objectionable. Indeed, the very existence of human institutions and governments represented for Lipscomb a profound departure from God's primordial design. In *Civil Government*, Lipscomb argued

---

[40] Lipscomb, GA (1890): 199.

[41] Lipscomb, *Civil Government* (hereafter CG) (Nashville: Gospel Advocate Pub. Co., 1889), 13-14, 16-17, 88-89, 91, 92,128,145.

that, from the beginning, God intended to be sovereign over all the earth. His sovereignty, in fact, formed the very essence of the Garden of Eden before the Fall. But "the act [by Adam and Eve] of . . . disobedience culminated in the effort of man to organise a government of his own, so that he himself might permanently conduct the affairs of earth, free from . . . God's government." This rejection of God's sovereignty meant for Lipscomb that humanity had transferred its allegiance from God to Satan. This, for him, was the meaning of Satan's statement to Jesus that all the kingdoms of earth "were delivered to me." For Lipscomb, then, human government was nothing less than Satan's dominion in rebellion against God.[42] Ever since humanity's rejection of God's government, Lipscomb claimed, God's intent had been to restore his sovereignty over the earth. This was the point of the Jewish wars against the Canaanite tribes. "The work to which they were called was a war of extermination against all people maintaining a human government." Again, God attempted a restoration with the advent of Jesus Christ into the world. At one level, Jesus' mission succeeded because he conquered "death and hell and the grave." At another level, however, Jesus' mission failed because it ultimately failed to destroy sin and rebellion.[43]

Precisely here Lipscomb introduced the same apocalyptic themes that characterized both Barton Stone and Tolbert Fanning before him. The day would come, Lipscomb claimed, when God would reestablish his sovereignty over all the earth and destroy all human governments, the best along with the worst. Like Stone and Fanning, Lipscomb also

---

42 Lipscomb, CG, 8-9, 48, 9-10.

43 Lipscomb, CG, 14, 46-47; "The Kingdom of God," GA 45 (May 21, 1903): 328; and CG, 51-53.

rooted this vision in Daniel, chapter two:

> The end of all the conflicts and strifes of earth, will be the complete and final destruction, the utter consuming of the last vestige of governments and institutions, and the giving of the dominion, and power, and authority of the whole earth to the people of the saints of the Most High. . . . All these kingdoms are to be broken in pieces, and consumed[,] . . . but the little stone cut out of the mountain without hands is to become a great mountain, and fill the whole earth.

Further, these themes for Lipscomb were the very "key notes . . . of the Old and New Testaments." Without them, the Bible was "without point of meaning."[44]

At this point, Lipscomb differed significantly, however, from his mentor, Tolbert Fanning, who had particularized the transcendent and had virtually identified the eschatological kingdom of God with the Church of Christ. Lipscomb agreed that, when God established the Church, he also reestablished his kingdom, rule, and authority. However, the kingdom of God in its church form was by no means the same as the eschatological kingdom that would break in pieces all the kingdoms of the earth. Lipscomb made this point abundantly clear in a key article he wrote in 1903 on "The Kingdom of God": "The kingdom in its present stage is not called 'the everlasting kingdom,' but it will grow into it. It is the same kingdom in a lower stage of growth and development." In *Civil Government*, he spoke of the church as the present manifestation of the coming kingdom of God. Like Stone before him, Lipscomb could not imagine final human perfection between the times of primordium and millennium.[45]

---

[44] Lipscomb, CG, 25, 27-28 (see also 83-84), 96.

[45] Lipscomb, "The Kingdom of God," GA 45 (May 21, 1903): 328; CG, 60.

Clearly, Lipscomb's apocalypticism embodied a profound eschatological expectation that governed his worldview. But was Lipscomb also premillennial? This question is important since premillennialism became such a pivotal issue for Churches of Christ during the first half of the twentieth century, and since Lipscomb's position on that issue was so hotly disputed following his death.

If by premillennial one means that, when Jesus returns, he will reign on the throne of David in Jerusalem for a literal thousand years, then Lipscomb apparently did not fit the description. In the first place, Lipscomb displayed little or no interest in the role of Israel and the throne of David in the millennial age. In the second place, Lipscomb always spoke of the kingdom of God "fill[ing] the whole earth, and stand[ing] forever."[46] The millennium for Lipscomb, therefore, was not a thousand-year interlude but rather the eternal rule of God on this earth.

However, if one means by premillennial simply that Jesus' return to earth will precede and inaugurate this final golden age, then Lipscomb clearly advocated a premillennial position. One finds glimpses of this position in an assortment of articles Lipscomb wrote for the *Gospel Advocate* over a period of years. For example, in 1878, Lipscomb commented favorably on the First American Bible and Prophetic Conference, convened at the Holy Trinity Episcopal Church in New York City in October of that year.[47] The speeches of the conference, he noted, focused on "the idea of the re-appearance of the Savior before and preparatory to the advent of the millenium [*sic*]," and he commended those speeches as doing "honor to the word of God." While Lipscomb was not then certain whether Christ's "coming precedes or succeeds the conversion of the world to God," he urged his readers to acquire copies of the speeches by writing to the New York *Tribune*, cautioning only that no one make this topic "a hobby to disturb the peace of churches."[48] Later

[46] Lipscomb, CG, 28.

[47] For this conference, see Timothy P. Weber, *Living in the Shadow of the Second Coming: American Premillennialism, 1875-1925* (New York: Oxford University Press, 1979), 28.

[48] David Lipscomb, "The Prophetic Conference," GA 20 (November 21,1878): 725.

in the century, Lipscomb spoke explicitly of a "reign of Jesus on earth" and declared that "'the times of restoration of all things' must be when Jesus returns again to earth—the restoration of all things to their original relation to God. . . ."[49]

Further, there can be no doubt that the millennium Lipscomb envisioned was a literal kingdom on this earth. Thus, for example, he spoke clearly of "the glorious millennial morn" in connection with "the re-establishment [of] the kingdom of God on earth." Again, he wrote, "the one purpose of God was to re-establish his authority and rule on earth." Or again, "This earth in the material, moral and spiritual world must become a garden of God's own planting." Further, to those who asked regarding God's rule on earth, "How would the mails be carried? How could the affairs of Railroads, Manufactures, and the many large corporations . . . be managed?" Lipscomb simply replied, "We will cheerfully commit the adjustment and management" of these things to God.[50]

Many in Lipscomb's circle shared these basic positions, though with differences in emphasis. James A. Harding, cofounder with Lipscomb of the Nashville Bible School, first president of that institution, and coworker with Lipscomb on the *Gospel Advocate,* candidly and explicitly advocated a view much more in keeping with classic premillennialism.

> When the saints are caught up to meet him, Christ comes with them to earth.... Satan is then caught, chained and cast into the abyss . . . [where] he is confined for one thousand years . . . [while] Christ and his saints reign; but the rest of the dead live not until the thousand years have expired. This, the resurrection of the righteous, is the first resurrection.

---

[49] David Lipscomb, "Queries," GA 37 (June 23, 1898): 397; and David Lipscomb, *Queries and Answers*, ed. by J. W. Shepherd (Cincinnati: F. L. Rowe, Publisher, 1918), 360.

[50] David Lipscomb, *A Commentary on the New Testament Epistles: Ephesians, Philippians, and Colossians*, vol. 4, ed. J. W. Shepherd, (Nashville: The Gospel Advocate Co., 1939), 76; Lipscomb, CG, iii, 28 (see also 12-13); and Lipscomb, CG, 136.

Others in Lipscomb's circle revealed time and again, often in an off-handed way, their premillennial assumptions. For example, when answering a question from a reader of he *Gospel Advocate,* E. G. Sewell simply assumed a millennium bounded by a "first resurrection" of the righteous and a "second resurrection" when "the thousand years of peace are finished." Phillip S. Fall—contemporary of Stone in Kentucky, close friend of Campbell, relative of Tolbert Fanning, and preacher for the Church of Christ in Nashville from 1858 to 1877—wrote to Mrs. Alexander Campbell:

> In regard to the pre-millennial advent, . . . the New Testament . . . impresses me with the hope that this earth . . . is to be the home of the righteous. . . . I can conceive of no higher ideal of heaven than that [we] . . . will dwell together with him . . . in this renovated spot. . . .[51]

Finally, Lipscomb and those in his circle strongly resisted elaborating on their premillennial perspectives and engaging in speculation regarding "what the millennium is or when it begins or ends."[52] They refused to speculate on the millennium because they did not wish to press beyond what they viewed as the bounds of Scripture. Further, they did not argue or debate the premillennial question simply because it was not an issue. Rather, it was a working assumption, one that characterized many in the Tennessee, Kentucky, and Alabama Churches of Christ from the days of Stone throughout the nineteenth century. In spite of all this, historians generally have failed to see that Lipscomb was

---

[51] James A. Harding, "The Kingdom of Christ versus the Kingdoms of Satan," *The Way* 5 (October 15, 1903): 929-31; E. G. Sewell, "Queries," GA 37 (July 11, 1895): 437; and P. S. Fall, "Interesting Reminiscences" [letter to Mrs. Alexander Campbell], GA 21 (May 15,1879): 310.

[52] See David Lipscomb, "Queries," GA 40 (June 23, 1898): 397; and Sewell, "Queries," 437.

premillennial at all.[53]

The third component in Lipscomb's anti-modern outlook was his rigorous pacifism and his refusal to vote or otherwise participate in civil government.[54] "The mission of the kingdom of God is to break into pieces and consume all these kingdoms, take their place, fill the whole earth, and stand forever," Lipscomb declared. "How [then] could the individual citizens of the kingdom of God found, enter into, and become part and parcel of—upbuild, support, and defend, that which God's kingdom was especially commissioned to destroy?" In this, Lipscomb by no means stood alone, for many premillennialists of his era embraced the same antipolitical posture and for precisely the same reasons. The Presbyterian dispensationalist James Brookes, for example, suggested that "those who are dead to the world and alive to

---

[53] Three factors help account for this oversight. First, the tendency of Disciple historians to understand their movement principally in terms of Alexander Campbell's faith in progress has obscured not only the premillennial sentiments of Stone but also those of Lipscomb as well. Second, the fervent refusal, especially of Lipscomb and his circle, to speculate on the Second Coming has led some to assume that he simply had little or no interest in millennial themes. Thus, for example, David Edwin Harrell argued that Lipscomb was "persistently unwilling to discuss the subject," something Harrell attributes to the general decline of interest in premillennial themes dating from before the Civil War. Harrell, *Quest for a Christian America*, 44, esp. n. 68. Third, beginning with World War I, Churches of Christ launched a frontal attack on premillennialism that lasted fully one-third of a century. When that attack had run its course by the mid-1940s, most mainstream Churches of Christ had come to view premillennialism as a heresy. Historians working within the context of the church, therefore, might well have little inclination to discern the significance of such views among revered leaders such as Stone and Lipscomb. Thus, both of Lipscomb's biographers—Earl West and Robert Hooper—simply ignore the premillennial theme in Lipscomb. West identifies the "kingdom" with the "church" and simply fails to see the apocalyptic dimension in Lipscomb's thought. See West, *The Life and Times of David Lipscomb* (Henderson, Tenn.: Religious Book Service, 1954), 97-99. Hooper spiritualizes Lipscomb's notion of the kingdom, suggesting that a "perfect kingdom," in Lipscomb's view, "could not be attained in this world," but only "in the world to come." Hooper, *Crying in the Wilderness: A Biography of David Lipscomb* (Nashville: David Lipscomb College, 1979), 110-22, esp. 121.

[54] Johnnie A. Collins has argued that Lipscomb's pacifism was principally a function of southern, post-Civil War sectionalism. Collins, "Pacifism in the Churches of Christ, 1866-1945" (Ph.D. diss., Middle Tennessee State University, 1984). That claim, however, is only partly true. In the first place, Lipscomb claimed that he arrived at these conclusions "early in life," long before the Civil War (CG, iii). In the second place, to ascribe Lipscomb's position only to the war is to diminish the importance of a long intellectual tradition that began with Stone and of which Lipscomb was heir. On the other hand, it is clear that the Civil War drove Lipscomb to take the Stoneite tradition seriously in a way he had not before. Indeed, Lipscomb cast his vote in 1860 for John Bell, the presidential candidate of the Constitutional Union Party (GA, 1912, 953). But he never voted again after the war.

Christ should avoid the polling place, because 'dead men do not vote.' "[55]

On the other hand, in perpetuating the old Stoneite worldview, Lipscomb stood fundamentally at odds with the Disciples of Christ of the late nineteenth century who perpetuated the Campbellian assessment of the world, modernity, and human progress. If Lipscomb had thought that the kingdom of God would "break into pieces" all the kingdoms of this earth, the editor of the Disciples-oriented *Christian Oracle* argued for "a very intimate relation between the advancing influence of Christian nations and the advancement of the kingdom of God." J. C. Tully typified the Campbellite/Disciples faith in progress when he asked, "Will the earnest desire in the hearts of men for freedom from the shackles of the past ever fade away and die?" and then rejoiced:

> Never, never, no never. The forces are going forward, not back. . . . So rapidly has the spirit of the age come upon us, that it may be affirmed of a truth: We are not in the same world, although on the same planet, with those who lived in the last century. We live in the age of progress in civilization and in all things which, in human judgment, minister to its perfection.[56]

These two opposing worldviews stood, in many ways, at the heart of the debates over missionary societies and

---

[55] Lipscomb, CG, 28 (see also 83-84 and iv); and James Brookes, "Gentile Dominion," *The Truth* 6 (1880): 536, cited in Weber, *Living in the Shadow of the Second Coming*, 92-93. Cf. J. J. Robinson, "Is Social Service Part of the Apostasy?" *Christian Workers Magazine* 14 (July 1914): 729-32, also cited in Timothy P. Weber, *Living in the Shadow of the Second Coming*, 92-93.

[56] J. C. Tully, "The Divine Law of Expansion," *Christian Oracle* 16 (January 18, 1899): 2; and J. C. Tully, "Responsibility of the Disciples of Christ to the Present Age," *Christian Quarlerly Review* 4 (1885): 581-82. For a brief discussion of the doctrine of Anglo-American progress among Disciples at century's end, see Harrell, *The Social Sources of Division in the Disciples of Christ*, 23-25. Harrell also notes that some Disciples leaders joined a postmillennial faith in American progress to prophetic themes.

instrumental music in the late nineteenth century and finally contributed to the emergence of two well-defined denominations: Churches of Christ and Disciples.

Indeed, when one understands Lipscomb's commitment to "the kingdom of God," one then can understand the genius of his restoration vision and why he took the positions he did on music, societies, and a host of other issues. If one imagines Lipscomb simply a legalist, committed only to restoring the forms and structures of the primitive church, then one has missed the heart of David Lipscomb. Lipscomb was a legalist, to be sure, but his legalism pointed beyond itself in two directions. First, it pointed to Eden before the Fall, when God's sovereign rule prevailed in sublime perfection. Second, it pointed to God's inevitable, final, and future rule over all the earth, when the perfections of Eden would be restored.[57] In between these times of perfection, the church was the finite manifestation of God's kingdom on earth. Moreover, because the restoration of the primordial and Edenic rule of God was absolutely certain, Christians must therefore live their lives and order their churches according to God's law in its every detail. In this sense, Lipscomb's efforts to restore biblical forms of worship and biblical patterns of church organization all pointed beyond themselves to the restoration of the kingdom of God in "the glorious millennial morn."

When this becomes clear, one also begins to see how Lipscomb could hold together in a single movement the modernizing heirs of Alexander Campbell and the anti-modern heirs of Barton W. Stone. The heirs of Stone fully understood the apocalyptic context of Lipscomb's legalism and his ethics. For them, rejecting instrumental music in worship and refusing to vote were two sides of the same apocalyptic coin. On the other hand, those who rooted their legalism in the biblicism of Alexander Campbell could simply ignore Lipscomb's apocalyptic thrust as well as his

[57] Lipscomb, CG, 136-37, 53-56.

position on civil government. If Lipscomb wanted to refuse to vote, that was an idiosyncrasy they could tolerate. For them, it was enough that Lipscomb railed against departures from the "ancient order" among the emerging Disciples of Christ.

During Lipscomb's lifetime, however, more and more of his people exchanged the anti-modern, apocalyptic vision of Stone for the rational, progress-oriented outlook of Alexander Campbell. Symptomatic of this shift was Lipscomb's lament in 1880 that a majority of the readers of the *Gospel Advocate* did not share his antipolitical position.[58] Those who made this shift would form the vanguard of Churches of Christ in the twentieth century. On the other hand, many who continued to hold the apocalyptic, anti-modern, and apolitical perspectives of Stone, Fanning, and Lipscomb would be cast from the mainstream as heretics.

## Postscript: The R. H. Boll Affair

Beginning in 1915 and continuing for one-third of a century into the 1940s, the emerging mainstream of Churches of Christ launched a sustained and, at times, ferocious attack against premillennial eschatology. The chief object of this attack for all those years was a German immigrant named Robert H. Boll, who enrolled in 1895 in the Nashville Bible School in Nashville, Tennessee. There he studied under James A. Harding and David Lipscomb, from whom he learned the separationist and apocalyptic perspectives that had energized many in Churches of Christ throughout the nineteenth century. Stridently anti-modern, Boll questioned whether "the boastful splendor of the twentieth century" and "the roar of its civilization" represented any serious progress at all. When the United States entered World War I in 1917, Boll counseled Christians to refuse to fight. He dismissed the notion that the war was "a struggle ... to make the world safe for democracy," grounding his counsel in the Stone-Lipscomb vision that the

[58] David Lipscomb, "Withdrawal," GA 22 (September 16, 1880): 597.

Christian simply does not belong to the kingdoms of this world.[59]

There is no question that Boll had learned his apocalyptic lessons from his teachers at the old Nashville Bible School, especially David Lipscomb and James A. Harding. At the same time, however, he expanded those themes to include the dispensationalism of proto-fundamentalists like Dwight L. Moody, Arno Gaebelain, Isaac M. Haldeman, Philip Mauro, James M. Gray, Reuben Torrey, W. E. Blackstone, and Cyrus I. Scofield—an outlook foreign to the nineteenth-century apocalyptic tradition of Churches of Christ.[60]

The battle against Boll marked the beginning of a great war on premillennialism that preoccupied and sapped the energies of preachers and editors in the emerging mainstream of Churches of Christ well into the 1940s. The question is, Why? Why the concern to destroy the premillennial sentiment when the mainspring of the Stone side of Churches of Christ had been anchored to a profoundly apocalyptic worldview that often had borne premillennial fruit throughout the nineteenth century? To call this turn of events ironic is, if anything, an understatement.

One is tempted to suggest that Churches of Christ made war on R. H. Boll because Boll had adopted a dispensational position with which Churches of Christ were largely unfamiliar. To some degree, that is true. The explanation is inadequate, however, both because dispensationalism was by no means the principal target of attack and because Churches of Christ rejected not just dispensationalism but the entire apocalyptic frame of reference.

Two reasons for this dramatic turnabout seem clear. First, Boll's premillennial outlook completely undermined the fundamental identity of Churches of Christ that prevailed in the early twentieth century, namely, the common

---

59 Robert H. Boll, "What Shall the End Be?" *The Way* 2 (April 1900): 60-61; and "The Christian's Duty As To War," *Word and Work* (hereafter WW) 11 (December 1917): 493-94.

60 Evidence abounds for the influence of dispensationalists on Boll. See, e.g., R. H. B., "About Books," WW 10 (February 1916): 88; "Bible Study Course," WW 10 (January 1916): 28; and "Jesus Is Coming," WW 10 (December 1916): 551. On Boll's dispensationalism, see R. H. Boll, *The Kingdom of God* (Louisville: Word and Work, n.d.).

conviction that Churches of Christ were identical, in all essential respects, to the churches of the apostolic age. Some, like Tolbert Fanning, Arthur Crihfield, and John R. Howard, had held this viewpoint since the late 1830s and early 1840s, but it blossomed in the early twentieth century as never before. This development was due in part to the fact that, between roughly 1880 and 1906, Churches of Christ passed through a bitter division with Disciples of Christ, who retained, in most locales, both the buildings and the majority of wealthy and influential members, especially in urban settings. In effect, Churches of Christ were left to begin all over again. Angered and defensive, Churches of Christ increasingly embraced the conviction that they, and they alone, were the true church, descended from the days of the apostles.

Boll's premillennial outlook, however, stood altogether at odds with this position. Boll argued, in fact, that the church most assuredly was *not* the kingdom of God in its fullness of perfection, either in its Pentecost beginnings or in its modern manifestation. Instead, that kingdom would come only in the last days when Christ would rule the earth with his saints. In the meantime, the church was a manifestation of that kingdom but was in no sense perfect or complete.

J. C. McQuiddy, publisher of the *Gospel Advocate,* typified the mainstream response when he charged that Boll's doctrine "belittles the church of Christ." Similarly, N. B. Hardeman complained that premillennialism made "the church of Christ absolutely an accident."[61]

Moreover, Boll provided a concrete demonstration of his own rejection of the sectarian exclusivism of Churches of Christ when he routinely ran articles from early fundamentalists like Gaebelain, Mauro, Torrey, and Blackstone on the pages of his journal, *Word and Work.* While most in the emerging mainstream of Churches of

---

[61] R. H. Boll, "Words in Season," WW 10 (July 1916): 338-39; and "The Olivet Sermon," WW 10 (November 1916): 487-92; J. C. McQuiddy, "Do the Kingdom and the Church Mean the Same Thing?" GA 61 (April 17, 1919): 367; and "Is the Church the Vestibule of the Kingdom?" GA 61 (March 20, 1919): 271-72; N. B. Hardeman, *Hardeman's Tabernacle Sermons*, vol. 4 (Nashville: Gospel Advocate Company, 1938),157.

Christ sympathized with the fundamentalists' fight against modernism, they nonetheless stood separate and apart from the formal fundamentalist movement for two reasons. First, they viewed the various denominations that fundamentalism represented as false churches. Second, they opposed the premillennial sentiments held by many in the fundamentalist camp as simply unbiblical. Typically, therefore, they viewed Boll's fraternization with fundamentalists as nothing short of scandalous.

Also prompting the loss of apocalypticism among Churches of Christ in the early twentieth century was a constellation of factors surrounding World War I. Popular pressure on all Americans to support the war was overwhelming, and Churches of Christ felt the pressure intensely. In the first place, support for the war was an obvious way for Churches of Christ to lift themselves from the position of social marginality that they occupied as a result of their rupture with the Disciples. In the second place, the United States government brought tremendous pressure on Churches of Christ to abandon their pacifist position in the interest of patriotism. The U. S. Attorney General for middle Tennessee, for example, threatened J. C. McQuiddy, publisher of the *Gospel Advocate,* with arrest if he continued to publish articles judged "seditious" and that discouraged "registration of young men under the Selective Service. . . Act." McQuiddy responded by halting all promotion of pacifism and all criticism of militarism on the pages of the *Advocate.* One observes among Churches of Christ from that date forward a gradual disintegration of the pacifist sentiment until, by the early 1960s, pacifism had almost entirely vanished from this fellowship.[62]

One witnesses the erosion during this period of not only pacifism but also the basic Stone-Lipscomb worldview that sustained the pacifist sentiment. Humpty Dumpty-like, the themes of apocalypticism, separation from the world, and reliance on the power of God rather than on human wit and

[62] F. W. Smith, "As a Matter of Simple Justice," GA 62 (September 23, 1920): 931. Cf. J. C. McQuiddy, "Conscientious Objectors," GA 59 (July 26, 1917): 720-21.

ingenuity all took a great fall, and all the preachers and all the editors would never be able to piece them together again with any semblance of coherence. In fact, for the most part, no one tried.

Thus, for example, while Stone, Fanning, and Lipscomb had held that human institutions were impotent to renovate the world and that God, at his initiative alone, would bring the millennial dawn, M. C. Kurfees now suggested that the League of Nations might well do God's bidding. "Who knows," he wrote, "but . . . [that the League's] adoption may be a long step toward the glad time when the nations 'shall beat their swords into plowshares, and their spears into pruning hooks;' and when 'nation shall not lift up sword against nation, neither shall they learn war any more.'" Moreover, if Stone, Fanning, and Lipscomb had embraced a fundamentally pessimistic view of human potential and progress, it was precisely that pessimistic outlook that the editors of the *Gospel Advocate* now sought to undermine. "It is not Christlike, it is not manly, it is not noble," McQuiddy complained in 1919,

> to sit down and whine that it is impossible to bring about such a condition [as the end of all war]. The same spirit would never have broken the Hindenburg line; the same spirit would never have conquered Germany and made her sue for peace. . . . The same spirit will never overcome the world, the flesh, and the devil, and bring the crown that is sure to come to the faithful.

Indeed, most *Advocate* editors no longer perceived tension between human civilization and the gospel. Instead, Western civilization was the fruit of the gospel. "Our civilization is its offspring," declared A. B. Lipscomb in 1914.[63]

---

[63] M. C. K., "The League of Nations and the Peace of the World," GA 61 (September 4, 1919): 866-67; J. C. M'Q., "The Peace League," GA 61 (March 27, 1919): 297-98; and A. B. Lipscomb, "Is Orthodox Christianity Today a Waning Power?" GA 56 (March 5,1914): 282-83.

If the "Boll issue" during World War I represented a rite of passage from Stoneite apocalypticism to Campbellian progressivism, Boll himself served as a surrogate target in the place of David Lipscomb. After all, Lipscomb was the "editor-bishop,"[64] a legend in his own time. No one dared attack David Lipscomb before his death or even for the twenty years following—no one, at least, who cared about his or her standing in the Churches of Christ. Further, almost no one was willing to recognize that Boll's teachers at the old Nashville Bible School—Lipscomb and James A. Harding—were chiefly responsible for Boll's apocalyptic worldview. Instead, Boll's opponents repeatedly charged that Boll derived his theology—lock, stock, and barrel—from Charles Taze Russell, founder of the Watch Tower Bible and Tract Society. This tactic clearly was an effort to discredit Boll, who denied any connection with Russell time and again.[65]

However, Lipscomb would not be able to escape attack forever. Indeed, by World War II, many who sought to accommodate themselves to modernity saw in Lipscomb and his theology a clear and obvious impediment to that transition. So long as his perspective was alive and well, Churches of Christ simply would be unable to join the modern world. Further, twenty years and more had elapsed since Lipscomb's death. The "modernists," therefore, imagined it was now safe to attack Lipscomb himself.

The man who more than anyone else engineered that attack was Foy E. Wallace, perhaps the most powerful person in Churches of Christ from the 1930s through the 1950s. A Texan, Wallace edited the *Gospel Advocate* from 1930 to 1934; he established his own paper, the *Gospel Guardian,* in 1935 for the express purpose of destroying premillennialism among Churches of Christ; and he founded yet another paper

---

[64] See Richard Hughes, "The Editor-Bishop: David Lipscomb and the *Gospel Advocate*," in *The Power of the Press: The Forrest F. Reed Lectures for 1986* (Nashville: Disciples of Christ Historical Society, 1986), 1-34.

[65] See, e.g., Cecil Douthitt, "Russellism Alias Bollism," *Bible Banner* (hereafter BB) 1 (September 1938): 13; and T. B. Wilkinson, "Heaven—the Kingdom—and Premillennialism," BB 6 (November 1943): 11. But cf. also R. H. Boll, "Studies in Prophecy: Some Distinctions Between Russell's Teaching and Bible Doctrine," WW 10 (July 1916): 312-15.

in 1938, the *Bible Banner,* where he launched stinging attacks on both premillennialism and pacifism.

Wallace's fundamental objection to premillennialism was the standard complaint that it undermined the restoration of true, apostolic Christianity and therefore also the identity and integrity of Churches of Christ. "The [Boll] theory," Wallace charged, "makes the church an accident, . . . the result of a prophetic default; a mere afterthought."[66]

Wallace himself had been a pacifist prior to World War II, but he underwent a conversion to militarism apparently due to Japan's attack on Pearl Harbor in December of 1941.[67] He immediately launched a withering attack on pacifists in Churches of Christ, labeling them as "men with a dwarfed conscience" and "freak specimen[s] of humanity."[68]

In 1942, Wallace opened the pages of the *Bible Banner* to an attack on David Lipscomb himself. W. E. Brightwell fired the first shot, noting that the pacifists in the church were only "those who have attended certain schools or have read a certain book [Lipscomb's *Civil Goverment*]." Brightwell simply could not fathom Lipscomb's claim that human government was the domain of Satan. "The purpose of civil government is good," he countered. "The devil does not have anything to do with it. The Lord does."[69]

Brightwell's comments reflect the extent to which World War I had indeed separated Churches of Christ from their nineteenth-century intellectual underpinnings. He, along with many others in Churches of Christ in this period, displayed a complete inability to fathom the Stone-Fanning-Lipscomb position that human institutions were flawed to the core. To

---

66 Foy Wallace, "What Is It All About—And What Difference Does It Make?" BB 1 (November 1938): 7; and "The 'New Spiritual Contingent Called "The Church"'—or, the Prophecies and Promises of God," BB 1 (August 1938): 3.

67 Foy Wallace, "The Government—Civil and Military," BB 4 (July 1942): 2; Glen E. Green, letter in "The Christian and the Government,"' BB 4 (July 1942): 7; and Cled Wallace, "What Pearl Harbor Did to Us," BB 6 (November 1943): 1.

68 Foy Wallace, "The Christian and the Government," BB 4 (March 1942): 8. Highly inflammatory, this article was unsigned. In July, however, W. E. Brightwell revealed that Foy Wallace had written the article, using Brightwell's notes. W. E. Brightwell, "For the Vindication of the Cause," BB 4 (July 1942): 6.

69 W. E. Brightwell, "For the Vindication of the Cause," 5, 7.

the contrary, government was good, especially the government of the United States. Minor defects may have existed, but the notion that government was fundamentally flawed, due to human sin, was for these moderns pure myth.

Perhaps no one reflected this new perspective more completely than did O. C. Lambert, who imagined government bad only if it did bad deeds. "I have been living sometime and the United States government has never persecuted me for my religion," Lambert crowed. "If that is the way the devil resists the church it seems to me he is wonderful." Lambert was simply incredulous that Lipscomb would make "the devil . . . the head of the United States government." Indeed, Lambert rightly pointed out, "Lipscomb recognizes no difference in the kingdoms. The United States government is just as bad as the rest. The government that gives so much freedom to Christians is no better than one that persecutes them."[70] Lambert simply stood amazed.

Though Lambert himself had earlier accepted Lipscomb's positions, he now announced, "I lose faith in the Lipscomb Lion and Lamb story!" Further, he felt certain that "the Lipscomb book would be outlawed now if the FBI knew its contents," and he encouraged Churches of Christ to "call all of them [copies of *Civil Government*] in and burn them."[71]

By October 1943, Wallace himself joined the attack and focused on the foundational apocalyptic perspectives of Lipscomb's *Civil Government*. "In looking back over the years in which this book and others like it were circulated among the brethren, it is not hard to see how the theories of Premillennialism found soil to grow among churches of Christ." Moreover, he rightly observed that "premillennialism calls for the very things that are taught in 'Civil Government' by David Lipscomb. The two theories go together; they fit each other perfectly." For these reasons, Lipscomb's book

---

[70] O. C. Lambert, "The David Lipscomb Book," BB 7 (September 1944): 9-10.

[71] O. C. Lambert, "The Lipscomb Theory of Civil Government," BB 5 (October 1943): 3; "The David Lipscomb Book," 15; "Canonizing Campbell and Lipscomb," BB 6 (May 1944): 10; and letter from Lambert in Foy Wallace, "The Lipscomb Theory of Civil Government," BB 6 (October 1943): 3.

was "about as rank with false doctrine as one book of its size could be," and Wallace expressed shame "that any recognized leader in churches of Christ, past or present, should espouse and promote such a doctrine" as that taught by David Lipscomb.[72]

By 1949, when he discontinued the *Bible Banner*, premillennialism—along with the entire apocalyptic worldview—was a lost cause among Churches of Christ except for a group of congregations loyal to this position and centered in and around Louisville, Kentucky, and New Orleans. Further, Wallace and his followers had convinced most members of mainstream Churches of Christ that premillennialists were badly deceived and perhaps even somewhat evil. Indeed, as early as 1944, E. R. Harper rejoiced that "R. H. Boll has been fought by every paper, pulpit, preacher and most schools," and that he and his people had been rejected "as unsound and therefore have been 'marked and avoided' by the church in general." He added, "The papers no longer allow him space to write his views and the pulpits are closed to him, . . . and most schools will not allow him to enjoy their fellowship."[73]

## Conclusions

By World War I, no one represented the old nineteenth-century "party of memory" more fully than did fundamentalists. Alienated from the modern world; suspicious of urbanization; resistant to the massive influx of immigrants foreign to the white, Anglo-Saxon, Protestant worldview; hostile to the intellectual developments of modernity, especially evolution, biblical criticism, and the scientific study of religion, fundamentalists yearned for an America of memory—or, perhaps, for a mythic America that never existed at all. The tension between these yearnings and

[72] Foy Wallace, "The Lipscomb Theory of Civil Government," BB 6 (October 1943): 6; " 'The Glorious Millennial Morn,' " BB 6 (May 1944): 5; and "The Lipscomb Theory of Civil Government," BB 6 (October 1943): 5.

[73] E. R. Harper, "Is It the Truth—Or the Person?" BB 6 (March 1944): 7.

the reality of modernity helped foster among many fundamentalists a premillennial eschatology that summoned the judgment of God on the kingdoms of this world. For the most part, however, the rest of America was marching triumphantly into the modern age, fighting a war to end all wars and making the world safe for democracy.

Given their nineteenth-century apocalyptic underpinnings, one would think that Churches of Christ would have stood shoulder to shoulder with fundamentalists, hurling judgment on proponents of modernity. It is true that Churches of Christ, due to their biblical primitivism, were deeply sympathetic with the biblicism of the fundamentalist movement. Yet, their exclusivism prevented them from formally joining the fundamentalists, and in their defense of human progress and their strident stand against apocalypticism, Churches of Christ unwittingly allied themselves with modernists with whom, ironically, they shared considerable common ground. Indeed, in opposing the apocalypticism of R. H. Boll, Churches of Christ joined hands with liberals like George Eckman, Shailer Mathews, Shirley Jackson Case, James Snowden, and George Preston Mains who were determined to drive premillennialism from America's churches.[74] In opposing Boll, Churches of Christ finally opposed the one person in their fellowship most in tune with the fundamentalist outlook and most at odds with the modernist worldview. Moreover, in opposing Boll, Churches of Christ separated themselves once and for all from the "party of memory" and aligned themselves decisively with the modernist "party of hope."

---

[74] George Eckman, *When Christ Comes Again* (New York: Abingdon, 1917); Shailer Mathews, *Will Christ Come Again?* (Chicago: American Institute of Sacred Literature, 1917), and *The Faith of Modernism* (New York: Macmillan, 1924); Shirley Jackson Case, *The Millennial Hope: A Phase of War-Time Thinking* (Chicago: University of Chicago Press, 1918), and *The Revelation of St. John: A Historical Interpretation* (Chicago: University of Chicago Press, 1919); James H. Snowden, *The Coming of the Lord: Will It Be Premillennial?*, 2d ed. (New York: Macmillan, 1919), and *Is the World Growing Better?* (New York: The Macmillan Co., 1919); and George P. Mains, *Premillennialism: Non-Scriptural, Non-Historic, Non-Scientific, Non-Philosophical* (New York: Abingdon, 1920). For a discussion of the modernist attack on premillennialism, see Weber, *Living in the Shadow of the Second Coming*, 117-21.

Even more, however, in opposing R. H. Boll and driving him from their fellowship, Churches of Christ brought to completion a shift in understanding of the restoration ideal that had been in process for at least a hundred years. Indeed, the anti-Boll and anti-apocalyptic crusade among Churches of Christ meant—at long last—that the *rational, progressive primitivism* of Alexander Campbell, fully in tune with the spirit of modernity, had emerged victorious over the anti-modern, *apocalyptic primitivism* of Barton W. Stone. In fact, it was only when Churches of Christ finally and decisively cut themselves loose from their nineteenth-century apocalyptic underpinnings that they could become friends of the modern world and allies of progress. From that time on, the mainstream of Churches of Christ faced itself in a decidedly modernist direction though, ironically, still professing its allegiance to a primitivist worldview.

# Critique and Analysis

**Douglas A. Foster**

The three essays you have just read are indisputably foundational for Stone-Campbell studies, though each has certain shortcomings. The process of engagement with and critique of the articles can in no way diminish their value but hopefully will aid readers to understand more fully the complex nature of this movement. Some of the matters mentioned merely point out how things have developed since the authors did their work. At other times there are more substantial matters. At still other points there are interesting comparisons and contrasts between the three essays.

Hatch, almost twenty years after Harrell, recognized the dual origins of the movement with the dual names—Christian and Disciples. It has been fairly standard in Stone-Campbell historiography to begin the story of the movement with accounts of the work of precursors Elias Smith, Abner Jones, and James O'Kelly, though usually with the caveat that their reforms did not go far enough. Hatch's grouping of these and the Stone and Campbell reforms into one "Christian Movement" makes good sense when slicing things the way he does. It becomes a real problem, however, when trying to make generalizations about them. He does acknowledge early that the different groups were a motley crew with few common characteristics, yet bases his article on the premise that they can be treated as one. Perhaps the clearest indication of overt differences between the groups, especially in what came to be called the Eastern Christians (Smith-Jones, O'Kelly) and the Western Christians (Stone), is the exchange of articles between the *Christian Palladium* and Barton Stone's *Christian Messenger*. As soon as news of the union of Stone and Campbell congregations in Kentucky and elsewhere reached the Eastern Christians, there was an immediate charge that Stone had left the original platform they had all occupied for many years. Campbell, they said, was a cold rational religionist, whose teachings would kill their efforts to revive and unite the churches. Stone defended his union with the Campbell reformation but was unsuccessful in persuading the Eastern Christians and many of the congregations in his own movement to enter it.[1]

This leads to another significant problem in Hatch's interpretation of Alexander Campbell. When speaking of his iconoclastic and populist tendencies, Hughes clearly indicates that he is speaking of the "early Campbell," a differentiation that Hatch does not make and which has generated some debate through the years.[2] Campbell begins to appear much more conventional than Hatch depicts him when one considers his founding and serving as President of Bethany College, and his urging the establishment of the movement's first national organization, the American Christian Missionary Society. As mentioned, the Eastern Christians strongly rejected what they saw as Campbell's rigidly structured theological system that they thought would kill both Spirit and Gospel. It would be hard to support the contention that Campbell understood "the people" to function in some kind of absolute way; rather, he saw the necessity of proper leadership and structure.[3] Hatch has at least partially

[1]See for example B. W. Stone, "Letter to Brother Badger," *Christian Messenger* 9 (May 1835):106-111; (June 1835):126-131; "Number III," *Christian Messenger* 10 (June 1836)81-83; "The Disunion of Christians," *Christian Messenger* 11 (March 1841):241-243; "Western Christians" *Christian Messenger* 11 (August 1841): 417-420; Marsh, "Cause of Division," *Christian Messenger* 11 (June 1841):336-338; B. W. Stone, "Reply to the Above," *Christian Messenger* 11 (June 1841):338-342.

[2]The assertion that Campbell was consistent on major theological positions throughout his career has come from two very different directions. Conservatives who saw Campbell as a model of strict biblical literalism and exclusivism rejected the idea that he had endorsed missionary organizations, claiming that he had become senile after the drowning death of his son Wycliffe in 1847, which left him easily manipulated by those favoring the societies. Campbell's biographer, Eva Jean Wrather, also insists that Campbell was consistent in his doctrinal stances, but this time on the matters of unity and Christian identity. Most historians, however, see a clear move from the early iconoclast to what Hughes calls an "irenic ecumenist." See Hughes, *Reviving*, 32-44, and Eva Jean Wrather, biography of Alexander Campbell, forthcoming.

[3]Eva Jean Wrather, *Creative Freedom in Action: Alexander Campbell on the Structure of the Church* (St. Louis: Bethany Press, 1968).

conflated Alexander Campbell and Barton W. Stone in his generalizations about early religious democratic ideas in the United States. Interestingly, a blurring of Stone's ideas into Campbell's, especially among writers in Churches of Christ, often occurred before the publication of the reprint edition of Stone's journal *The Christian Messenger* by Star Bible Publications in 1978,[4] the publication of which served to delineate differences in the two mens' views on a variety of topics.

Two minor matters. The first concerns Hatch's description of Stone as a zealous Calvinist early in life and his later rejection of that system for "gospel liberty" (p. 27). This is true at one level. However, though Stone did embrace Calvinism in a sense at his initial conversion, he seems always to have been conflicted by much of what he regarded as fatalism in Calvinism.[5] In addition, Stone retained important parts of Calvinism throughout his life, including a strong sense of God's sovereignty and human inability, what Hughes calls an "apocalyptic" world view.[6] Second, Hatch has his dates slightly off regarding two events of Stone's early career: Stone withdrew from the Synod of Kentucky with his colleagues to form the Springfield Presbytery in 1803, not 1802; and the Last Will and Testament was written in 1804, not 1803 (p. 17).

[4]See for example the thirteen-lesson series on Stone by L. L. Brigance in the 1933 volume of the *Gospel Advocate*. For discussions of changing perceptions of Stone in the twentieth century see Anthony L. Dunnavant, ed., *Cane Ridge in Context: Perspectives on Barton W. Stone and the Revival* (Nashville: Disciples of Christ Historical Society, 1992).

[5]Stone admits in his autobiography that in 1798 at his ordination he still taught that human beings "were so totally depraved that they could do nothing acceptable to God, till his Spirit, by some physical, almighty, and mysterious power had quickened, enlightened, and regenerated the heart, and thus prepared the sinner to believe in Jesus for salvation." Yet he also shows that he had had doubts about the doctrines of election, reprobation and predestination for some time. *The Biography of Eld. Barton Warren Stone, Written by Himself: With Additions and Reflections by Elder John Rogers* (Cincinnati: J. A. & U. P. James, 1847) 29, 30.

[6]D. Newell Williams, "Barton W. Stone's Calvinist Piety," *Encounter* 42 (Autumn 1981):409-417; Richard T. Hughes, "The Subversion of Reforming Movements," pp. 41-58 in *Founding Vocation and Future Vision: The Self-Understanding of the Disciples of Christ and the Churches of Christ* (St. Louis: Chalice Press, 1999) 55-56.

In contrast to Hughes, Harrell completely ignores influences from the Stone part of the movement. He identifies two contrasting tendencies that eventually split into Disciples and Churches of Christ, describing them as legalistic restorationists and those promoting a denominationally oriented unity emphasis. He identifies the differences as sociological and psychological—reflecting his earlier work at Vanderbilt University and the two seminal volumes that resulted from it.[7] Harrell's identification of restoration and unity as the two impulses to which Churches of Christ and Disciples laid their respective claims has been a standard interpretation for some time.[8] Yet subsequent work has shown that judgment to be inadequate as an explanation for the divisions in the movement. Hughes and others have pointed out complex varieties of restorationism as well as understandings of Christian unity within the movement itself that preclude any simple "unity vs. restoration" dichotomy.[9]

Harrell's use of the terms "liberal" and "conservative" is problematic. To use the label "liberal" for Isaac Errett and most of the people associated with the *Christian Standard* is to use it in a sense other than theological. Opposing or supporting instruments and societies was not in itself an indication of theological conservatism or liberalism. Many who supported those "innovations" in the movement's first division were true theological conservatives who later separated from liberal Disciples to form what some would

---

[7]"A Decade of Disciples of Christ Social Thought" (M.A. thesis, Vanderbilt University, 1958); "A Social History of the Disciples of Christ to 1866" (Ph.D. thesis, Vanderbilt University, 1962); *Quest for a Christian America: The Disciples of Christ and American Society to 1866* (Nashville: Disciples of Christ Historical Society, 1966); *The Social Sources of Division in the Disciples of Christ, 1865-1900* (Atlanta: Publishing Systems, Inc., 1973).

[8]See for example Winfred Ernest Garrison and Alfred T. DeGroot, *The Disciples of Christ: A History* (St. Louis: Christian Board of Publication, 1948) 338-339, 550-552; James DeForest Murch, *Christians Only: A History of the Restoration Movement* (Cincinnati: Standard Publishing, 1962), 265-266; Thomas J. Liggett, "Why the Disciples Chose Unity," *Mid-Stream* 19 (April 1980): 227-233.

[9]Richard T. Hughes and C. Leonard Allen, *Discovering Our Roots: The Ancestry of Churches of Christ* (Abilene, Texas: ACU Press, 1988); Douglas A. Foster, "The Struggle for Unity During the Period of Division of the Restoration Movement, 1875-1900" (Ph.D. thesis, Vanderbilt University, 1987).

call a "fundamentalist" body.[10] Though Harrell acknowledges the terminology problem with the three historic names–Christian Churches, Disciples, and Churches of Christ—he does not adequately recognize the tendencies already in existence in the late nineteenth century that would lead to the separate identity of independent Christian Churches.

Harrell's object here is to examine the reasons for the predominantly southern character of Churches of Christ. He contends that the specific issues (instruments and missionary societies) were incidental–other issues would have divided Disciples if it had not been these–because the real source of division was social, not theological, and the chief social issue was slavery. This was a significant insight for many in the movement. The predominant historiography, from Moses Lard's article "Can We Divide?" to the standard histories in the mid-twentieth century,[11] had denied any major impact on the movement by the issues surrounding the Civil War.[12] One problem with Harrell's explanation is that his focus on sectional differences resulting from the Civil War tends to leave the impression that the differences were recent and not already solidly in place in the ante-bellum period. Hughes focuses on the theological and ideological differences that existed well before the Civil War as the source of division, yet he acknowledges the truth of Harrell's sociological arguments as far as they go.

In many ways Hughes remedies some problems in the other two articles, correcting, for example, Harrell's neglect of Stone and Hatch's conflation of Campbell and Stone. Yet Hughes opens up his own set of difficulties in this brilliant

[10]James Brownlee North, "The Fundamentalist Controversy Among the Disciples of Christ, 1899-1930," (Ph.D. Thesis, University of Illinois at Urbana-Champaign, 1973).

[11]Moses E. Lard, "Can We Divide?" *Lard's Quarterly* 3 (April 1866):330-336; Garrison and DeGroot, *The Disciples of Christ: A History*, 330.

[12] Bill Humble was another historian of the movement who was among the first to recognize the major role of sectional issues in the division. Bill J. Humble, "The Influence of the Civil War," *Restoration Quarterly* 8 (Fourth Quarter, 1965):233-247; "The Missionary Society Controversy in the Restoration Movement," Ph.D. thesis, State University of Iowa, 1964.

essay. Hughes's point is that while elements of Campbellite rationalism and Stoneite apocalypticism had been fused early in the roots of Churches of Christ, the group had progressively excised the authentic Stoneite character for a "modern" or rationalist identity in a series of twentieth century events—seen here in the R. H. Boll incident and developed more fully in his 1996 history of Churches of Christ.[13]

One of the things that makes Hughes's essay so striking is his portrayal of the profound irony of a conservative, even fundamentalistic, religious body that came to embrace "modernist" notions about human ability. Churches of Christ, Hughes contends, exchanged their heritage of utter reliance on God and submission to his will for a worldview that elevated the ability of humans to discern and conform to the mind of God through rational processes.

Two problems arise from this premise. First, though more implied than explicit in this article,[14] Hughes assumes that the Stone-Campbell Movement had captured at its beginning the right worldview (at least its apocalyptic part). Churches of Christ, he contends, lost that perfect vision in the twentieth century, but can and ought to recover it. Interestingly, this idea seems to embody many of the very attitudes Hughes criticizes in the optimistic "modern" worldview of Alexander Campbell. It is, in a sense, an appeal to restore the early Restoration Movement through a program that itself seems still to rely heavily on modern notions of human ability to get it right again.

The other problem has to do with the assertion that modernist attitudes "triumphed" in Churches of Christ in the early twentieth century. There is no doubt that the rational, modern, optimistic attitude became a major characteristic in Churches of Christ—or remained so as part of the Campbell legacy. Yet Churches of Christ have always been diverse. The

---

[13]*Reviving the Ancient Faith: The Story of Churches of Christ in America* (Grand Rapids, Mich.: W.B. Eerdmans Pub. Co., 1996).

[14]See Hughes's "The Taming of the Restoration Tradition," in *Founding Vocation*, 59-74.

rationalistic worldview was never totally triumphant in this complex and variegated body. Hughes himself provides some evidence of this in *Reviving the Ancient Faith,* telling stories of leaders like K. C. Moser and E. H. Ijams, and of groups like the one-cup, non-class and non-institutional churches. The work of Michael W. Casey on the continuing pacifist tradition in Churches of Christ provides ample evidence of such "apocalyptic" elements in Churches of Christ.[15]

Hughes is undoubtedly right when he contends that "modernism" as he defines it has been a powerful force—perhaps the most powerful—in twentieth-century Churches of Christ. What he fails to say explicitly is that equally powerful elements that contradict and challenge this modernism have always been present as well.[16] The realization of this truth makes Hughes's final verdict less conclusive than it may first appear.

With all of that said, one can only reiterate the immense importance of these three studies and hope that by engaging them readers will have a greater sense of the work that still needs to be done on this rich historical tradition.

---

[15]See for example Michael Wilson Casey, "Warriors Against War: The Pacifists of the Churches of Christ in WWII," *Restoration Quarterly* 35 (July 1993):159; "Pacifism in the Restoration Movement: 1954-1945 to the Present," *Gospel Advocate* 136 (December 1, 1994):28.

[16]For an excellent treatment of a number of these "other voices" throughout the history of the Stone-Campbell Movement see C. Leonard Allen, *Distant Voices: Discovering a Forgotten Past for a Changing Church* (Abilene: ACU Press, 1993).

# GENERAL HISTORIES OF THE STONE-CAMPBELL MOVEMENT

I. Written by members of Churches of Christ

A. Earl I. West, *The Search for the Ancient Order: A History of the Restoration Movement*. Indianapolis: Religious Book Service, 1949- . 4 vols. (Vol. 1 1800-1865; vol. 2 1866-1906; vol. 3 1900-1918; vol. 4 1919-1950.)

B. Leroy Garrett, *The Stone-Campbell Movement: An Anecdotal History of Three Churches*. Joplin: College Press, 1981; revised ed., *The Stone-Campbell Movement: The Story of the American Restoration Movement*. 1994.

C. Richard Hughes, *Reviving the Ancient Faith: The Story of Churches of Christ in America*. Grand Rapids: Eerdmans, 1996.

II. Written by members of Independent Christian Churches

A. James Deforest Murch, *Christians Only: A History of the Restoration Movement*. Cincinnati: Standard Publishing, 1962.

B. Henry E. Webb, *In Search of Christian Unity: A History of the Restoration Movement*. Cincinnati: Standard Publishing, 1990.

C. James B. North, *Union in Truth: An Interpretive History of the Restoration Movement*. Cincinnati: Standard Publishing, 1994.

III. Written by members of the Christian Church (Disciples of Christ)

A. Winfred Ernest Garrison and Alfred T. DeGroot, *The Disciples of Christ: A History*. St. Louis: Bethany Press, 1958.

B. William E. Tucker and Lester G. McAllister, *Journey in Faith: A History of the Christian Church (Disciples of Christ)*. St. Louis: Bethany Press, 1975.

C. Mark G. Toulouse, *Joined in Discipleship: The Maturing of an American Religious Movement*. St. Louis: Chalice Press, 1992. Also the revised edition, *Joined in Discipleship: The Shaping of Contemporary Disciples Identity*. St. Louis: Chalice Press, 1997.